GCSE

The Curious Incident of the Dog in the Night-Time

Mark Haddon
ADAPTED BY **Simon Stephens**

Notes and activities: Julia Waines
Series consultant: Peter Buckroyd

Oxford Literature Companions

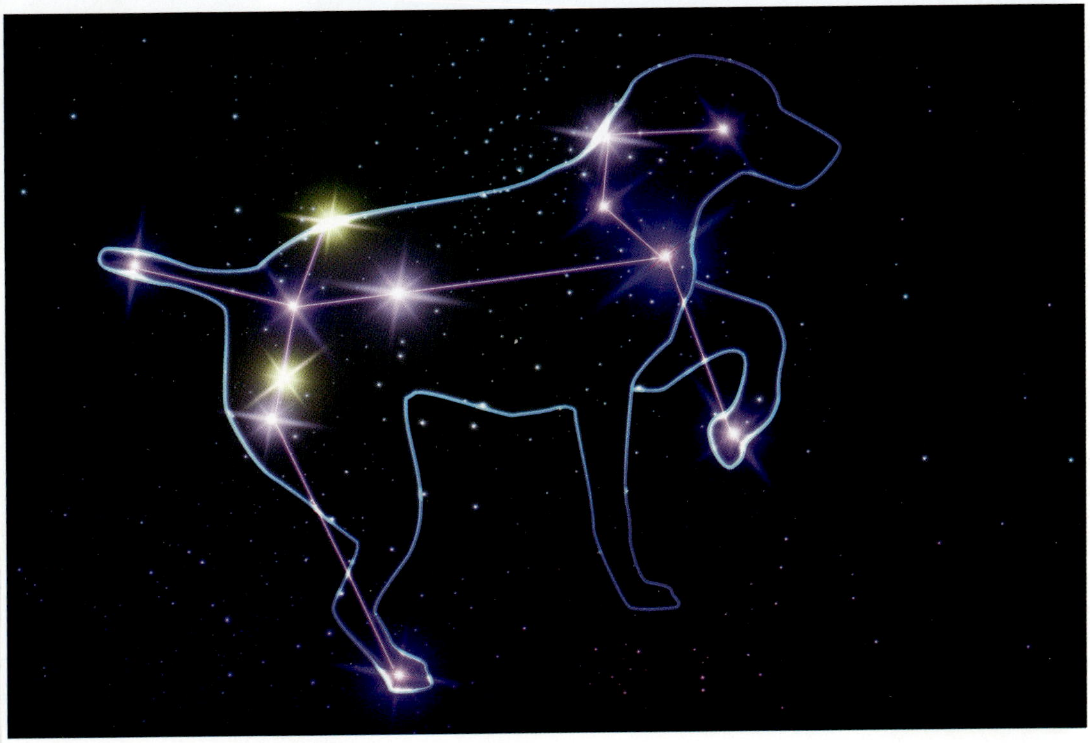

Contents

Introduction	4

Plot and Structure — 6
Plot	6
Structure	25

Context — 28
Biographies	28
Historical and cultural context	29
• Education of students with disability or special educational needs	29
• History of autism	32
• City life	33
Literary context	36

Characters — 38
Main characters	38
• Christopher	38
• Ed	40
• Judy	43
Minor characters	45

Language — 52
Realistic tone	52
Swearing	52
Humour	54
Christopher's language	55
Use of the first person	56
Sentence structure	57

Themes — 60
Honesty and truthfulness — 60
Difference — 62
Family relationships — 63
Science and maths — 65

Performance — 68
Creating the roles — 68
- Physicality — 68
- Unconventional movement — 70
- Voice — 72
- Timing — 73

Staging — 73

Skills and Practice — 76
Exam skills — 76
- Understanding the question — 76
- Planning your answer — 78
- Writing your answer — 81

Sample questions — 86
Sample answers — 88

Glossary — 95

Introduction

What are Oxford Literature Companions?

Oxford Literature Companions is a series designed to provide you with comprehensive support for popular set texts. You can use the Companion alongside your play, using relevant sections during your studies or using the book as a whole for revision.

Each Companion includes detailed guidance and practical activities on:

- **Plot and Structure**
- **Context**
- **Characters**
- **Language**
- **Themes**
- **Performance**
- **Skills and Practice**

How does this book help with exam preparation?

As well as providing guidance on key areas of the play, throughout this book you will also find 'Upgrade' features. These are tips to help with your exam preparation and performance.

In addition, in the extensive **Skills and Practice** chapter, the 'Exam skills' section provides detailed guidance on areas such as how to prepare for the exam, understanding the question, planning your response and hints for what to do (or not do) in the exam.

In the **Skills and Practice** chapter there is also a bank of **Sample questions** and **Sample answers**. The **Sample answers** are marked and include annotations and a summative comment.

How does this book help with terminology?

Throughout the book, key terms are **highlighted** in the text and explained on the same page. There is also a detailed **Glossary** at the end of the book that explains, in the context of the play, all the relevant literary terms highlighted in this book.

INTRODUCTION

Which edition of the play has this book used?

Quotations have been taken from the Bloomsbury edition of *The Curious Incident of the Dog in the Night-Time* (ISBN 978-140-817335-0).

How does this book work?

Each book in the Oxford Literature Companions series follows the same approach and includes the following features:

- **Key quotations** from the play
- **Key terms** explained on the page and linked to a complete glossary at the end of the book
- **Activity boxes** to help improve your understanding of the text
- **Upgrade** tips to help prepare you for your assessment

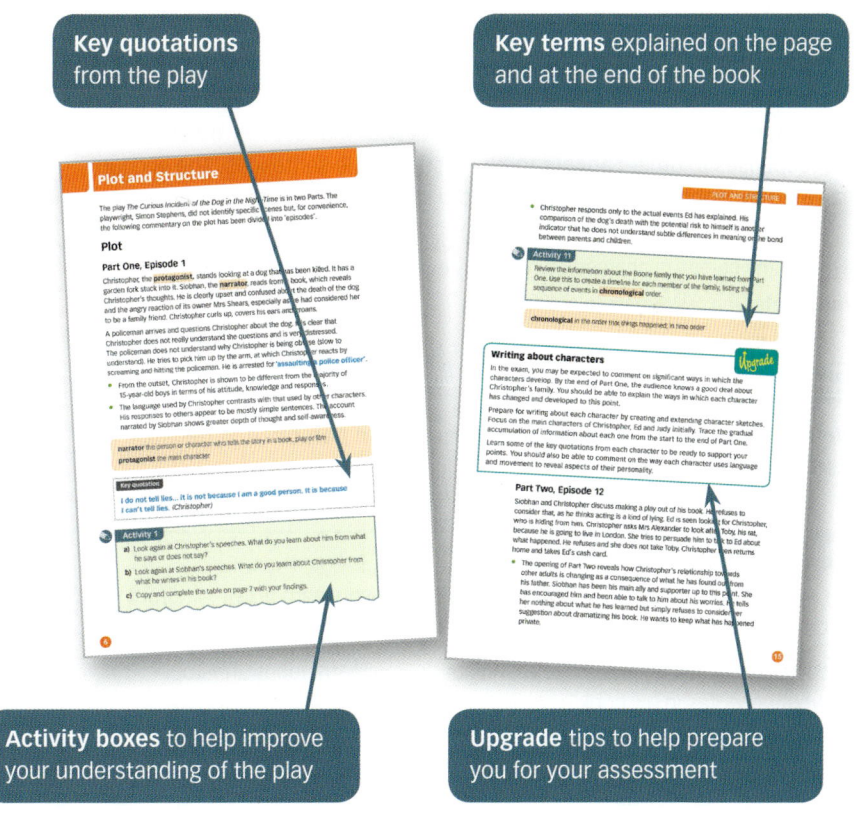

Key quotations from the play

Key terms explained on the page and at the end of the book

Activity boxes to help improve your understanding of the play

Upgrade tips to help prepare you for your assessment

Plot and Structure

The play *The Curious Incident of the Dog in the Night-Time* is in two Parts. The playwright, Simon Stephens, did not identify specific scenes but, for convenience, the following commentary on the plot has been divided into 'episodes'.

Plot

Part One, Episode 1

Christopher, the **protagonist**, stands looking at a dog that has been killed. It has a garden fork stuck into it. Siobhan, the **narrator**, reads from a book, which reveals Christopher's thoughts. He is clearly upset and confused about the death of the dog and the angry reaction of its owner Mrs Shears, especially as he had considered her to be a family friend. Christopher curls up, covers his ears and groans.

A policeman arrives and questions Christopher about the dog. It is clear that Christopher does not really understand the questions and is very distressed. The policeman does not understand why Christopher is being obtuse (slow to understand). He tries to pick him up by the arm, at which Christopher reacts by screaming and hitting the policeman. He is arrested for **'assaulting a police officer'**.

- From the outset, Christopher is shown to be different from the majority of 15-year-old boys in terms of his attitude, knowledge and responses.
- The language used by Christopher contrasts with that used by other characters. His responses to others appear to be mostly simple sentences. The account narrated by Siobhan shows greater depth of thought and self-awareness.

> **narrator** the person or character who tells the story in a book, play or film
> **protagonist** the main character

> **Key quotation**
>
> **I do not tell lies... it is not because I am a good person. It is because I can't tell lies.** *(Christopher)*

Activity 1

a) Look again at Christopher's speeches. What do you learn about him from what he says or does not say?

b) Look again at Siobhan's speeches. What do you learn about Christopher from what he writes in his book?

c) Copy and complete the table on page 7 with your findings.

PLOT AND STRUCTURE

What you learn from Christopher	What you learn from Siobhan
He struggles to cope with other people. He does not respond to Mrs Shears.	He is very precise: 'It was seven minutes after midnight'

Part One, Episode 2

Christopher is taken into custody. He has to empty his pockets but, when the Duty Sergeant tries to remove his watch, he starts screaming again. He is allowed to keep it. Christopher's father Ed arrives and they are interviewed about the death of the dog. Christopher repeats that he does not lie and did not kill the dog. He is given a police caution. Siobhan discusses with him why people can be confusing.

- When Ed arrives, he uses finger touch only with Christopher. This is clearly all that Christopher can cope with and something that is not understood by the police, hence his extreme reaction.
- Christopher does not show any understanding of non-verbal communication.
- Another feature of Christopher's language is the **literal** nature of his responses. He appears to take questions or statements at face value and shows no understanding of **inference** or **imagery**.

imagery the use of visual or vivid language to convey ideas or emotions
inference the working out of something by using evidence and applying reasoning
literal using and understanding words in their most obvious meaning

Activity 2

Look at the speeches in this episode from **'Do you have any family Christopher?'** to **'Do you know your father's phone number Christopher?'**

- How do these show that Christopher and the Duty Sergeant are talking about slightly different things?
- How is humour created by this misunderstanding?

PLOT AND STRUCTURE

Part One, Episode 3

Ed and Christopher go home. Christopher decides he should try to find out who killed the dog, which was called Wellington. Ed does not agree: **'It's a bloody dog'**.

Siobhan reads about the day that Christopher found out his mother had gone into hospital. He was told by Ed that she had a problem with her heart and that he was not able to visit her.

Christopher decides to investigate who killed Wellington

- The relationship between Ed and Christopher is shown to be quite tense. Ed appears brusque or offhand with his son. His comments are mostly in the form of instructions and show that he expects Christopher to do as he is told.
- While recounting the death of his mother, Christopher provides the audience with a detailed breakdown of every step of his day, including details that most people would not register. His attention to even these trivial details reveals more about the way his mind differs from that of most other 15-year-olds.

Activity 3

Christopher is very concerned about the killing of Wellington; Ed is not. Copy and complete the table below to show their different attitudes. Try to use quotations to support your points.

Idea	Christopher's view	Ed's view
Speaking to Wellington	'... I went to say hello...'; Christopher thinks of Wellington as a friend even though he was a dog.	'... keep your nose out...'; Ed thinks the events should be nothing to do with Christopher and wants him to stay away.
Finding out who killed Wellington		
Murder should be investigated		
Dogs are as important as people		
The death should make people unhappy		

PLOT AND STRUCTURE

Part One, Episode 4

Siobhan and Christopher discuss him writing a story about the death of Wellington. Christopher says he knows he is going against his father's wishes. He complains that sometimes people do not make sense in the instructions they give him. Ed tells Christopher that his mother has had a heart attack and died. He cannot give any further details. Christopher tries to talk to Mrs Shears about her dog, but she is not receptive and doesn't want to know about his ideas. Christopher asks Reverend Peters, the vicar who visits school, to tell him where heaven is. The vicar is unable to provide an answer that Christopher understands.

- The action in this episode moves about in time from the 'present' (when Wellington's death occurred) to the 'past' (when Christopher's mother died). This may be intended to convey the idea that in Christopher's mind the two events have similar significance. He appears to have been equally affected by both events.

- Adults are seen to find Christopher difficult to deal with. He does not respond in expected ways to comments and his answers suggest he is not aware of the **subtext** in what is said: *'Can you go now Christopher'*. His very factual understanding of the world can be seen as both a strength and a weakness of his personality.

subtext an underlying idea or thought

Activity 4

This episode shows Christopher interacting with Mrs Shears and Reverend Peters, two adults who know him less well.

Focus on the conversations Christopher has with Mrs Shears and Reverend Peters. How does Stephens show that they know him less well? Write about:

- the ways each adult deals with Christopher's questions
- the ways Christopher responds to each adult
- how Stephens makes Christopher look more mature/knowledgeable with each of them.

Key quotations

Ed: Christopher, I'm sorry your mother's died. She's had a heart attack. It wasn't expected.

Christopher: What kind of heart attack?

Part One, Episode 5

Christopher speaks to neighbours as he tries to find out who killed Wellington. Ed stays in to watch football on TV. No one can tell Christopher anything useful. Number 40 remarks that perhaps Christopher needs to speak to his father rather than undertaking independent investigation. Christopher is seen to be nervous around people he does not know well: **'I don't talk to strangers'**. He is also seen to be anxious about social situations: **'I don't go into other people's houses'**.

- Despite his social awkwardness, it is clear that Christopher is known by the local community. The responses from the neighbours show that they recognize him and are concerned for his welfare: **'You be careful young man'** and **'Do you want to come in for tea?'** He is better known than he realizes and there is an implied understanding of his difficulties.

- Stephens is building an expectation in the audience that Ed knows more about situations than Christopher realizes. The reference to Mrs Shears being sad and who may be responsible for that carries a certain inference that Christopher misses entirely. His narrow view of the world is seen by the audience as limiting his understanding of relationships and emotions.

Activity 5

What do you learn about Christopher from his interactions with his neighbours?

a) Copy and complete the table for each of the three main encounters.

b) Then write a paragraph on each encounter.

Neighbour	What is learned about Christopher from their conversation?
Mr Thompson's brother	Christopher does not recognize that the person he is speaking to is not his neighbour, but his neighbour's brother. This could suggest that he does not know the neighbour very well or that he does not recognize faces.
Number 40	

Part One, Episode 6

Christopher applies logic to reason through the killing of Wellington and concludes that Mr Shears is the most likely suspect. Meanwhile, Ed argues with the headteacher of Christopher's school that he should be allowed to take Maths A level: **'Jesus, this is the one thing he's really good at'**.

Later, Ed confronts Christopher about his enquiries into Wellington's death. The tension rises when Christopher shares his suspicions about Mr Shears and

Ed reacts with extreme anger. He makes Christopher promise to stop working on the problem. Siobhan and Christopher share his dream about becoming an astronaut. It is clear that Ed finds the whole discussion difficult.

- Christopher has clearly given the idea of being an astronaut a great deal of thought. His detailed description of life inside a space module reveals more about the difficulties he faces with 'normal' life: **'Sometimes when I want to be on my own I get into the airing cupboard and… pull the door closed behind me…'**. Neither Siobhan nor Ed appears to be disturbed by this comment, which shows that they both accept and are not worried about this type of behaviour from Christopher.

- The character of Ed is becoming more complex as the play progresses. Stephens presents him as being a strong advocate for Christopher, publically supporting him, but at the same time being impatient and angry with him. He is a three-dimensional character with his own concerns and issues, which the audience also wants to learn more about.

Activity 6

What does the audience learn in this episode about Christopher from his fantasy about becoming an astronaut? Make notes in answer to the following questions.

a) Pick out the aspects that Christopher clearly sees as advantages because of his social communication difficulties.

b) What do the facts about space that he includes in his explanation reveal about him?

c) Why is the final phrase, **'Dream Come True'**, capitalized?

Tips for assessment

In exam responses to characters, you will need to be able to show the ways in which characters develop through the text. Your comments should be supported by quotations or references to the different points in the plot at which change or development can be identified. Prepare for this by learning short quotations about the main characters.

Part One, Episode 7

Christopher tells Siobhan about the conversation with Ed and having to promise to stop investigating Wellington's death. He is worried about the culprit still being at large, but Siobhan encourages him to do as he promised. Mrs Alexander speaks to Christopher again. He shares that he is going to do an A level in Maths despite being in a special school. When asked about Mr Shears, Mrs Alexander suggests that Christopher should speak to his father.

PLOT AND STRUCTURE

In the course of the discussion, it becomes apparent to the audience that Mrs Alexander knows more about the 'death' of Christopher's mother than he does. They go to the park in order to discuss the matter. Mrs Alexander reveals that Mr Shears had been having an affair with Christopher's mother. Shocked, Christopher leaves abruptly and goes home. He does not tell his father what he has learned.

- Christopher's innocence in terms of adult relationships is highlighted as he fails to pick up on the inferences being made about his mother's relationship with Mr Shears. The series of questions he asks shows his naivety and inability to understand implication.
- Mrs Alexander is the **catalyst** for Christopher starting to become more aware of reality as opposed to him simply accepting at face value what he has been told about his mother.

catalyst someone or something that triggers events

Activity 7

Mrs Alexander says, **'I'm not a stranger… I'm a friend'**. Write a short paragraph on whether you agree with this statement or not.

a) Consider to what extent her revelations are 'friendly' towards Christopher.

b) What motives can you suggest for her revealing what is clearly local knowledge to Christopher?

Part One, Episode 8

Siobhan and Christopher talk about what he has found out about his mother. He has written it all in his book. While this is happening at school, Ed finds the book and reads what Christopher has written. Christopher recounts an episode he recalls about being at the seaside with his mother Judy.

Ed confronts Christopher about what he has learned from the book. Ed is very angry and accuses his son of ignoring what he was told to do. They fight and Christopher is hurt. Ed apologizes and tries to explain his reactions. Christopher's main concern, however, is where his book has gone.

- The language Ed uses to Christopher is shocking for the audience but reflects the level of frustration and anger Ed feels. His calmer response after the fight also reveals how strongly Ed feels that he is responsible for Christopher and how he worries about his son's future.
- The episode with Judy provides an insight into the sort of person she was. This is the first scene where she appears as a character rather than simply as a recollection. Her fantasy life – **'If I hadn't married your father…'** – is far removed from the reality of living with Christopher.

> **Activity 8**
>
> Siobhan asks, **'What was your mother like Christopher?'**
>
> **a)** What does the audience learn from his answer?
>
> **b)** Create a character profile of Judy based on the information in this section.

Part One, Episode 9

Christopher explains to Siobhan about the fight with Ed. She reads the section of his book where he gives a detailed account of his attempts to find his book again. He does find it in Ed's wardrobe but also discovers a shirt box containing a lot of letters all addressed to him. He guesses they are from his mother due to the distinctive way she writes.

- The repetition of **'detected'** in this episode reveals the way Christopher regards his search for his book. This is consistent with his earlier assertions about investigating Wellington's death.
- It could be assumed that **dramatic irony** starts to be seen in this episode. The audience will make the links between Judy having 'died' and the appearance of letters from her as an indication that she is actually still alive somewhere.

> **dramatic irony** a situation where the audience knows more than the characters

> **Activity 9**
>
> Read Siobhan's speech where Christopher describes looking for his book from **'When I got home from school…'** to **'… to buy shirts in them'**. Focus on the words Stephens has chosen to use.
>
> Identify three features of the language that show Christopher's attitude to finding his book. You could use the starter sentences below to help you:
>
> *Stephens repeats the word 'detected' to emphasize that Christopher considers himself to be doing valid investigation work. Using the word so frequently has the effect of showing that Christopher's vocabulary is…*

Part One, Episode 10

Ed wants to put up shelves, so Christopher uses this as an excuse to shut himself in his room and read the letters he has found. Judy voices these. At first, Christopher is not sure they are actually from his mother. He tells Ed about his day only in response to direct questioning. He does not mention the letters. Ed goes out and Christopher has the opportunity to read all 43 letters. They reveal the difficulties the family coped with as Christopher was growing up and Judy's own feelings of ineptitude as a parent. Christopher is overwhelmed with the amount of emotion and information he has absorbed. He curls up on the floor and vomits.

- Christopher is seen to be able to use the truth selectively in order to conceal what he is really doing. He gives Ed partial information about his day. This is a development from the scene with Mrs Alexander when he omitted to mention that he knew the truth about his mother. This increasing capacity to hide the truth could be regarded as an indication that Christopher is learning to deal with the adult world.
- Judy is shown to have had real struggles with knowing how best to deal with Christopher. She considers that Ed has more patience with him and her own role is shown to diminish as he gets older.

> **Activity 10**
>
> Look again at the stage directions in this episode starting **'As Judy reads so Christopher…'** and **'Christopher continues to build…'**. Write a paragraph about what Christopher's behaviour and movement are intended to show the audience about his state of mind.

Part One, Episode 11

Ed returns to find Christopher lying in his own vomit and the pile of opened letters. After sorting out clean clothes for Christopher, he pours out his reasons for having lied to him for two years: **'You have to know that I am going to tell you the truth from now on. About everything'**. He also admits to having killed Wellington in a fit of temper after rowing with Mrs Shears. Christopher decides he can no longer stay at home with Ed as he feels it is unsafe. He considers who he could live with instead. His only choice appears to be going to find Judy in London.

- The broken structure of Ed's speeches shows his state of mind. He is trying to explain his motives in language Christopher will understand but is also struggling with the emotional implications of what he has allowed his son to believe.

Ed finds Christopher collapsed and surrounded by the letters, a crisis point that prompts him to tell his son the truth

- Christopher responds only to the actual events Ed has explained. His comparison of the dog's death with the potential risk to himself is another indicator that he does not understand subtle differences in meaning or the bond between parents and children.

Activity 11

Review the information about the Boone family that you have learned from Part One. Use this to create a timeline for each member of the family, listing the sequence of events in **chronological** order.

chronological in the order that things happened; in time order

Writing about characters

In the exam, you may be expected to comment on significant ways in which the characters develop. By the end of Part One, the audience knows a good deal about Christopher's family. You should be able to explain the ways in which each character has changed and developed to this point.

Prepare for writing about each character by creating and extending character sketches. Focus on the main characters of Christopher, Ed and Judy initially. Trace the gradual accumulation of information about each one from the start to the end of Part One.

Learn some of the key quotations from each character to be ready to support your points. You should also be able to comment on the way each character uses language and movement to reveal aspects of their personality.

Part Two, Episode 12

Siobhan and Christopher discuss making a play out of his book. He refuses to consider that, as he thinks acting is a kind of lying. Ed is seen looking for Christopher, who is hiding from him. Christopher asks Mrs Alexander to look after Toby, his rat, because he is going to live in London. She tries to persuade him to talk to Ed about what happened. He refuses and she does not take Toby. Christopher then returns home and takes Ed's cash card.

- The opening of Part Two reveals how Christopher's relationship towards other adults is changing as a consequence of what he has found out from his father. Siobhan has been his main ally and supporter up to this point. She has encouraged him and been able to talk to him about his worries. He tells her nothing about what he has learned but simply refuses to consider her suggestion about dramatizing his book. He wants to keep what has happened private.

- The taking of the cash card is a further step along Christopher's path to increasing maturity. It is the first time he has shown awareness of the need to deal with money and that he will need it to achieve his plan of going to London.

> **Activity 12**
>
> Christopher has consistently applied logic to the situations he has encountered.
>
> a) It could be argued that Christopher's assertion, '**... Father lied to me. And also he killed Wellington and so that means he could kill me**', is both logical and illogical. Draw up a table to record your views.
>
> b) Consider what Christopher's assertion reveals about his understanding of emotions. Write up your ideas using the table to help you explain your views.

Part Two, Episode 13

Christopher embarks on his journey to find Judy. He seeks help from people who fail to perceive his difficulties. He appears overwhelmed by the quantity of information he has to process at the train station. He is helped to withdraw cash and buy a ticket by a policeman but then struggles to locate the platform. In his head, he hears Siobhan explaining how to tackle the problem of going to the right place.

- The Voices in this section represent the sensory input that Christopher is receiving. This sensory input is mainly auditory (what can be heard). The variety of instructions, suggestions, adverts, appeals and information represents what people deal with when travelling by train but, unlike Christopher, most people will also only pay attention to them in a selective way. The majority of people can filter this information so they only hear/read what they are interested in. Christopher cannot do that.

- Understanding language is difficult for Christopher. He is not aware of how **sarcasm** or **colloquialisms** are used. Although this creates an element of humour for the audience, it creates confusion for Christopher and his only recourse is to ask questions or repeat statements until he receives an answer that makes sense to him.

> **colloquialism** informal or slang language
>
> **sarcasm** a **tone** of voice often used in a mocking way, suggesting that the speaker is not sincere
>
> **tone** mood or attitude

PLOT AND STRUCTURE

Activity 13

How does the conversation between the Station Policeman and Christopher show the teenager's limited experience of the wider world? Identify four points that reveal his lack of understanding. Write about each point, explaining how Stephens uses it to show the audience how limited Christopher's experience is up to this point.

Part Two, Episode 14

The Station Policeman detains Christopher on the train. He explains that Ed is looking for him and wants Christopher to get off the train. Christopher refuses and screams when the policeman tries to take his arm. He continues to refuse until the train moves out of the station, trapping the policeman with him. The policeman's plan is to leave the train at Didcot, with Christopher. After going to the toilet, Christopher climbs into the luggage rack to hide. When the train stops, he is accosted by people collecting their luggage. Then he decides it is safe for him to get off the train. The noise of the busy station is overwhelming again.

- From the list Christopher gives of what he can see out of the train window, it is clear that he experiences more than auditory overload. He lists all the things he spots, observing even insignificant details at the same time as more obvious ones. This seeing of every part simultaneously appears to create chaos in his mind as he is unable to 'filter out' what is unnecessary or irrelevant to him.

Other members of the cast lie on the floor to give the impression that they are in their train seats while Christopher is hiding in the luggage rack

PLOT AND STRUCTURE

- Hiding in the luggage rack is consistent with what the audience already knows of Christopher. He has already said that, when stressed, he will hide in a small place until he feels safe and calm enough to come out. In this episode, he also has to deal with a range of different people approaching him. No one appears unduly concerned about him being there and all continue about their own business.

- The reappearance of the Voices contributes to Christopher experiencing sensory overload, which means he has to stop and try to calm down. The dramatic focus is to show the audience how the world might be experienced by people with **autism**. Stephens deliberately shows how the sheer amount of information bombarding Christopher in different forms makes it is difficult for him to take in and fully understand it. It is clear how hard it might be for Christopher to choose the appropriate piece of information from the whole lot.

Autism

Autism is a developmental disorder that affects people in different ways. It is present from birth and often impacts on a person's ability to understand and communicate with other people. For more information, see the section 'History of autism' on page 32 in the Context chapter.

Activity 14

Observation is a way of looking at situations or events, and gathering as much information about them as possible. Look in detail at Christopher's comments about observation in this episode from **'I see everything…'** to **'"Jane plus Ian 4 ever"'**.

Compare Christopher's approach to observation with that of 'lazy' observers. How does Christopher's observation differ from 'lazy' observation? What do we learn about Christopher from this section?

Part Two, Episode 15

Christopher finds out how to get to the address where his mother lives in Willesden. It is obvious that he has limited experience in dealing with people. While trying to deal with the confusion of the tube (London Underground), he imagines a conversation with Ed about what he is doing. It is clear that Christopher is learning what to do by observing other people. His father seems to have little

Christopher learns to negotiate the tube in London

faith in his ability to succeed as his comments are mainly negative. Christopher is clear that he no longer considers his home to be with Ed.

- The series of questions that Ed poses represents the self-doubt that Christopher is experiencing. By characterizing these doubts, Stephens is showing how Christopher struggles to cope with his **internal dialogue**.
- Observation is shown to be a key learning tool for Christopher. He knows **'To watch the people. It's easy look...'**. He relies on what he sees others doing and then copies them. This is a basic learning technique. What surprises the audience is how long Christopher needs to do it and how he needs to articulate what he sees in order to understand it.

Activity 15

What do you learn about Christopher's relationship with his father from the conversation in this episode? Look back at the notes you have already made about Ed. Add further points from this episode. Consider the level of negativity Ed shows about what Christopher is doing and the ways he shows concern about Christopher.

internal dialogue a discussion held in a person's mind; a way to think about aspects of a problem before arriving at a conclusion

mantra words repeated to help concentration

Part Two, Episode 16

Christopher listens to Ed to understand how to get onto a tube train. He watches the process for a while before realizing that Toby has escaped from his cage. He sees him on the rail line, so climbs down to catch him. Members of the public are horrified and, as a train approaches, try to get Christopher to come back. He is unaware of the danger and, having rescued his rat, gets back on the platform. He still needs to catch the train but the pressure of the crowds takes the choice from him and he is carried into the carriage.

- Christopher talks to Toby in the same way that parents might speak to a disobedient child. This shows that Christopher does not differentiate between humans and animals in the same way that most people do and this is consistent with his reaction to Ed having killed Wellington.
- The spoken repetition of the pattern of events as trains arrive and leave – **'Train coming. Train stopped. Doors open. Train going. Silence.'** – reinforces the learning style Christopher needs to be able to function. Ed repeats this twice, then Christopher continues the **mantra** eight times before he can move.

PLOT AND STRUCTURE

Activity 16

Look back over the interactions Christopher has with various people at the tube and train stations. How do these add to your understanding of the difficulties he faces when he has to deal with people who do not know him? Write two paragraphs, one each about how Christopher responds to:

- the role of 'officials' (station guard, information)
- members of the public (punk girl, man with socks) he encounters.

Part Two, Episode 17

Christopher is unable to find out if he is on the right train, but the speaking directions show that he is. When he gets off the tube, he struggles to find the way to his mother's flat and buys an A–Z of London. He becomes overwhelmed by the whole adventure and, because Judy is not in, ends up squatting in a ball by her door. Judy and Roger arrive in the middle of a row and find Christopher, soaking wet and bewildered by what he has done. Judy is amazed. Christopher is more worried about Toby being fed than himself. They go into the flat. Christopher tells Judy that Ed had said she had died, which comes as a shock to her.

Christopher waits for his mother to come home to her flat

- The first time Judy and Roger are seen as a couple they are having a dispute: **'... you made me look like a complete idiot'**. This suggests that the relationship is not as harmonious as Judy's letters said. It may also suggest that the relationship has deteriorated since the pair had left their former partners to live together.

- Judy is unsure what to make of Christopher arriving at her door and is obviously amazed he has made the journey alone. Several things suggest how distant she feels from Christopher: she has forgotten that he doesn't like to be touched; she asks him a number of questions that he is unsure how to answer; her emotional response echoes the way Christopher behaves: **'She starts to howl'**.

- Roger's response to finding Christopher borders on aggression: **'What the hell is going on?'** This could be due to his shock at finding Christopher outside the flat or worry that Ed is also there and a confrontation with him is imminent.

PLOT AND STRUCTURE

Activity 17

In this episode, Christopher is seen to be almost emotionless. He responds to Judy's questioning in very straightforward ways. He is shown to be unaware of the impact of his appearance, what he has done and what he says.

Write a short paragraph in response to each of these questions:

- What impact does this lack of emotion have on the audience?
- What reasons can you suggest for Christopher being shown like this, when previously, whilst travelling, he was shown experiencing fear and worry?
- What impression does the audience have of the adults in this scene?

Part Two, Episode 18

The London Policeman interviews Christopher because he had been reported as a runaway. Judy and Christopher confirm that he wants to stay in London. Ed arrives and has a confrontation with Roger and Judy. He tries to talk to Christopher, who uses his knife to show he is afraid of his father. He does not speak to Ed. The police return, having been called by Roger, and persuade Ed to leave. Christopher sleeps.

- Christopher has locked himself in the bedroom. This may reflect the insecurity and uncertainty he feels about being in a new place. Being with his mother does not appear to provide the reassurance he is seeking. That might be due to the presence of Roger Shears, who is a 'stranger' to him.
- Ed's exasperation and worry are evident from the conversations he has with Judy and Christopher. Roger is a largely ignored irrelevance. Ed justifies his lies about Judy dying and is sarcastic about her commitment to her son.
- The audience realizes that the portrayal of Christopher has been from a sole perspective until this point – his own. The revelations from Ed create a different image of Christopher and show the much broader range of issues that Ed has had to deal with alone. Judy's leaving now starts to look more like the act of a woman who could not cope any longer, rather than one who simply had an affair.

Key quotation

I cooked his meals... I worried myself sick... I went to school every time he got into a fight. And you? *(Ed)*

PLOT AND STRUCTURE

Activity 18

Judy and Ed are seen together for the first time in the play.

a) What can be deduced about Judy and Ed's past and present relationship from the way they speak to each other and Christopher in this episode? The starter below may help you:

Judy is immediately confrontational with Ed about the lies he has told Christopher about her. 'What in God's name...' sounds like the continuation of a row that began a long time ago. It is almost as if they have never been apart...

b) Write down three other things that are apparent about their relationship. Use quotations to support your points.

Part Two, Episode 19

Christopher appears to be manipulating his mother into behaving how he expects. He reveals that he needs to return home to do his A level Maths exams. He is seen, unable to sleep, wandering in the street outside the flat. He is talking to Siobhan in his head when his mother finds him. Judy and Roger struggle to work out how to care for Christopher. Judy has lost her job and has told Christopher's school that he will not be returning to do his exam. Christopher reacts badly. He refuses to read library books Roger has brought and is later almost assaulted by Roger when he is drunk.

- Judy, though caring deeply for Christopher, fails to recognize his manipulation or to deal with what he says about Roger. She also fails to understand the importance of the A level Maths exam he is due to take. Her approach to resolving these problems focuses on her own needs. She is seen to be emotionally fragile and lacking in confidence in her own ability as an adult and a parent.
- After this episode, Roger does not appear in the play again. His interactions contribute to the final outcome and resolution of the events.

Activity 19

a) Look at the information you have about Roger Shears. Create a character profile of him based on **hearsay** evidence as well as interactions with other characters.

b) Do you think he is meant to be a bad person? Justify your answer with reference to sections of the text.

hearsay information that comes from another character and has not necessarily been witnessed by the audience

PLOT AND STRUCTURE

Tips for assessment

Knowledge about the minor characters in the play as well as the main characters will be necessary for a full understanding of the drama. In an exam, you may be expected to write about two or three of these minor characters and their impact on the events. You should make sure you learn at least one quotation from each minor character to use when writing about them.

Part Two, Episode 20

Judy and Christopher leave the flat at 4 a.m. to go back to Swindon because Judy fears the situation could become worse in London. They go to Ed's house and he leaves so that Christopher can settle. Now home, Christopher demands to do his A level Maths exam as scheduled. Judy speaks to the headteacher to arrange it. The exam is reorganized at short notice, but Christopher is initially so stressed that he cannot understand the questions. Reverend Peters calms him so he can tackle them. Siobhan intervenes afterwards to stop Christopher telling the audience how to solve a particular problem.

- It is clear from Siobhan's reaction that she has never met Christopher's mother until she needed to reschedule the exam: **'So you're Christopher's mother...'**. This could be seen as another indication that Judy struggled to cope with parenting Christopher and backs up Ed's point about how much responsibility fell on his shoulders.

- Siobhan speaks to Christopher about the audience of the play not wanting to hear about a maths problem and its solution. This is called **'breaking the fourth wall'**. The characters are showing awareness that they are part of a play. They remain in role but are addressing the audience as well as each other.

breaking the fourth wall when characters speak directly or show that they are aware of the audience

Activity 20

Compare and contrast the roles of Siobhan and Judy. You could consider:

- In what ways do they each contribute to Christopher's development?
- How do they deal with Christopher when he finds situations difficult?
- What does the audience learn about each woman's personality?

Create a mind map to show the roles of both characters in Christopher's life.

PLOT AND STRUCTURE

Part Two, Episode 21

Christopher speaks to Ed about the exam, which is the first time they have spoken since he ran away. He tells Siobhan about the flat he is living in with Judy and the difficulties of sharing facilities with other lodgers. He spends some time at Ed's house until Judy returns from work but he finds that even more difficult because he doesn't trust Ed. He barricades himself into his old room. Ed takes steps to rebuild their relationship by buying Christopher a puppy. It has to stay at Ed's. Christopher gets an A* for his Maths exam and explains to Siobhan how things are improving for him with Ed and for his plans for the future.

- The end of the play shows how Christopher has developed so that he has confidence in himself for his future. He has clear plans and knows he can tackle the obstacles because he has already done something similar. The character has progressed in unexpected ways.
- The relationship with Siobhan is still the most stable and secure one that Christopher has. She is the person with whom he is sharing his plans at the end; she is the person that he asks, **'Does that mean I can do anything do you think?'** The question is posed to the audience as much as to Siobhan. We are challenged to reconsider our own views of his difficulties and how our expectations of someone may limit that person.
- The stage directions at the end of this episode are surprising in their tone. This may be to convey Stephens's view that it is important for Christopher to be able to do something that he feels is significant, even if that is beyond the mathematical abilities of most of the audience!

Activity 21

Consider the ways in which Christopher's expectations of his life have become more realistic.

a) Compare what he said about becoming an astronaut in Part One, Episode 6 with what he says about becoming a scientist at the end of Part Two, Episode 21. Consider the following questions.

- What differences are there between these plans/dreams?
- What reasons can you suggest for the change?
- How has Stephens used language to show the differences?

b) Write a paragraph dealing with each question.

Maths Appendix

Christopher addresses the audience directly and explains how he will use the stage technology to make clear how he answered the maths question about a right-angled triangle. He uses a timer to show how he solved it in six minutes. He goes through the question, breaking it down to show how the Greek mathematician Pythagoras's theorem was correct.

- The stage directions again suggest Stephen's sense of humour: *'(... lasers if you have the money, or holograms if you are in the future)'*.
- The language in the final episode is completely different to that in the rest of the play – less about thoughts and feelings, but factual and precise in what is being explained. This is perhaps to reflect the way that Christopher's mind works.

Activity 22

Read the maths question and its answer. Why do you think Stephens chose to end the play with a complex, A-level standard mathematical problem that many members of the audience would not understand? Write a paragraph to explain what Stephens may have been trying to show.

Structure

The play is divided into two parts. Each part deals with different times of Christopher's life:

- Part One deals with the killing of Wellington and Christopher's decision to find out who did it. It is set mainly where Christopher lives or at his school.
- The interval falls at the point when Christopher makes the decision to go to find where Judy lives.
- Part Two shows the consequences of what he has found out about Wellington and the steps he takes to secure his future. This part is set mainly on the journey to London and in the Willesden flat. The very end of the play is again set in Swindon at Christopher's home and school.

PLOT AND STRUCTURE

Activity 23

a) Create a tension graph based on Part One of the play. Include up to eight events and place them chronologically but also in relation to the level of tension the audience will feel. Use the example below, completing it with your own choice of events.

b) Which event did you scale as most tense? Explain your reasons.

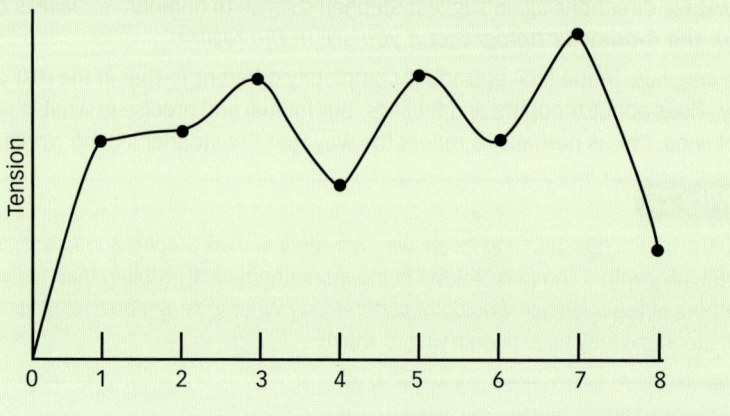

The play has a circular structure as it begins and ends in the same place when Christopher is having a discussion with Siobhan.

The timeline across the whole play is not consistent. At some points, the audience is aware that they are being shown **flashbacks** but at other points the action appears to be reflecting Christopher's mind. At the start of the play, the time appears compressed – a lot of events occur close together. Towards the end, the time is more extended and covers the period between Christopher taking his exams and getting the results some months later.

The play is also episodic. This is a technique that is sometimes associated with playwrights like the 20th-century German playwright Bertolt Brecht. The events that are shown are all linked together by the character of Christopher – he is on stage for the whole play and everything that happens is seen from his perspective. There are no clear divisions between the different parts of the play as the action flows from one event to the next.

flashback a scene set at an earlier point than the main story

Stage directions are used minimally, which enables the **director** to make choices about the ways that characters move or interact. The stage directions that are provided tend to focus the attention of the audience on the ways in which Christopher reacts to other characters. The structure appears quite open, meaning that a director can choose how they want the characters to move about rather than being 'tied' to a specific instruction from the author.

Writing about plot and structure

You need to be able to show that you understand the plot and how it is structured. It has been written specifically to make the maximum impact on the audience.

Remember:

- how the story is organized and sequenced by Stephens so that the audience can understand events clearly
- the way pieces of information are given over time to build tension and anticipation
- the chronological order of events, as well as other techniques like **foreshadowing**.

Check your knowledge of the plot and structure.

1. Create a timeline of the story. First, break it down into events in chronological order.
2. Under the chronological timeline, create another timeline to show the order in which events happen or are revealed in the play.
3. Finally, write a paragraph to explore why Stephens chose to make the plot non-chronological and suggest the effect this has on the audience.

---

director the person who supervises and controls the development of the performance

foreshadowing a literary **device** that hints at what will happen later in the story

device a technique used for a particular purpose

Context

Biographies

Mark Haddon wrote the original novel on which the play was based.

- Mark studied at Oxford University and then Edinburgh University.
- He has had a number of jobs, including working with people with learning disabilities.
- He writes for teenagers and younger children as well as for adults.

Simon Stephens wrote the play as an **adaptation** of the novel.

- Simon began his career writing at the Royal Court Theatre.
- He has written a large number of other plays for stage, TV and radio.
- He has won a number of awards for his plays, including one in Germany.

The Curious Incident of the Dog in the Night-Time was Haddon's first novel, for which he won two literary awards

> **adaptation** a piece of work that has been changed for a different purpose

Stephens's stage play won the Olivier Award for Best New Play

CONTEXT

Activity 1

The table below outlines some of the issues Stephens faced when turning the original novel into a play.

a) Copy and complete the table with your ideas about why these might have been problems for him.

b) Try to add at least one more issue to the table.

Issue	Why this might have been a problem
Novel is written in the first person.	Showing just one point of view of events might be hard on stage when there are so many other characters who speak and interact with Christopher.
A lot of the novel is about what Christopher thinks.	
Much of the novel is dialogue, with some description of places and people.	
In the novel, events happen in non-chronological order.	

Tips for assessment

You will not need a detailed knowledge of the background of either Haddon or Stephens to be successful in the exam. You should not refer to it unless you are showing how it may have affected how they wrote.

Historical and cultural context

The novel was written in 2003 and the play adaptation was first seen in 2012. Set in the same time period, the play shows a range of issues associated with living in the early 21st century.

Education of students with disability or special educational needs

One of the main aspects of context that comes out of the play is the way that Christopher lives and is educated in 21st-century Britain.

CONTEXT

Until late in the 19th century, education for children with special educational needs (SEN) or disabilities was not compulsory. Schools may have tried to include children with SEN but, until 1893, when the government introduced laws for the education of blind and deaf children, this was a matter of choice for each school. More legislation followed over the next 50 years:

- Elementary Education (Defective and Epileptic Children) Act 1899 – local authorities had to provide for the training of physically and mentally disabled and epileptic children
- Education Act 1918 – education became compulsory for the physically disabled
- Education Act 1921 – compulsory education for children with these disabilities extended to 16
- Education Act 1944 – established that children's education should be based on their age, aptitude and ability. Eleven categories of 'handicap' were described, which included 'educationally subnormal' and 'delicate' as well as blind.

Children with any type of difficulty or disability were largely treated as if they had a medical condition and so their education was the responsibility of the Medical Branch of the Board of Education after it was established in 1907. Special schools were sometimes regarded as stigmatizing and creating further difficulties with integrating into society. Mrs Alexander tells Christopher, **'I see you every day, going to school on your school bus'** *(Part One)*. Although they both live on the same street, they have never spoken because Christopher is transported to and from school, and has not had contact with any of his neighbours.

Between 1974 and 1978, Baroness Warnock conducted a review of special educational needs (SEN) and disabilities in England and concluded that 20% of the school population might be regarded as having some SEN or disability, but only 2% of students actually needed the provision of special schools to help them learn. The majority should expect to be taught within a mainstream school setting. This led to the first Education Act in 1981, which detailed what local authorities would be expected to do in order to meet the educational needs of students with disabilities or learning difficulties. This Act has been amended and extended several times since then in order to improve education for all students in an appropriate school.

A key feature of schools in the 21st century is that they become 'inclusive' places to learn. Baroness Warnock used this idea in 2005 when she called on the government to rethink the ways that students with additional needs were educated. She suggested that new types of special schools should be created, which enabled some students with similar needs to be educated together. However, this should only be for students with the most significant needs as the majority would benefit from remaining in mainstream schools with specialist provision to enable them to succeed in the same way as their friends and peers from the local community.

Stephens portrays Christopher as one of the very few students who needs special school provision, though it is not made clear to the audience exactly why this is the case. The special school appears to cater for students with very different levels

CONTEXT

SEN students learning about social skills and emotions in a modern special school

of need. His own mathematical ability seems an odd contrast to his peers' abilities when he reports to Ed that one of his classmates has struggled to understand the purpose of a toilet and another '… **probably couldn't even fetch a stick'** *(Part One)*. The needs of these young people are completely different, yet there seems to be no alternative but to educate them together. Baroness Warnock suggested that inclusion (in mainstream schools) can make students feel physically included but socially and emotionally isolated and excluded.

 ### Activity 2

a) Do you think Christopher benefited by attending a special school? Think about issues connected with friendships, how children learn to behave in society (socialization) and educational differences.

b) Copy and complete the table below with evidence from the text and your own experience of education. The first entry has been done for you.

Benefits of attending special school	Disadvantages of attending special school
Smaller class sizes means that Christopher can have more attention and support for his learning.	Christopher is gifted at maths. He may not be able to have teaching at the right level to help him progress as the staff will not be experienced in teaching A level.

CONTEXT

History of autism

In recent years, many more people have become familiar with the term 'autism' to describe a particular type of behaviours or developmental disorders. However, it was first identified in the early 20th century and it is a subject that continues to stimulate research and new discoveries about the condition.

Stephens presents Christopher so that the audience assumes him to have the milder form of autism known as Asperger syndrome due to his unusual ability with maths and his obsessive interest in science. His determination to investigate Wellington's death is part of his obsessive behaviour, which is unaffected by Ed telling him to stop.

Christopher is also seen as being quite unemotional. He deals with events by asking questions until he has satisfied his interest. The answers are treated very rationally and the only events that appear to trigger an emotional reaction are when he is touched. He does not appear to be upset even when told that his mother has died. However, this could be seen as a feature of the difficulty autistic people sometimes experience as they are unsure of how to react to an emotional event. It may be that they need extra time to process their reactions before being able to explain them. Christopher does react at once to the news that Ed killed Wellington because he no longer feels safe with his father. Stephens shows that Christopher is able to make decisions based on an emotional event even though his choice of reaction may not be the same as other young people of a similar age.

> **Key quotation**
>
> I don't feel sad about it because Mother is dead... So I would be feeling sad about something that isn't real and doesn't exist and that would be stupid. *(Christopher, Part One)*

Activity 3

Some employers now actively seek to recruit employees with autism to work on particular projects. Using the evidence from the play, write a short answer to each of the following questions:

- What aspects of Christopher's autism would make him a good employee?
- In what ways might his workplace need to be adapted to help him succeed there?

CONTEXT

Tips for assessment

You will need to demonstrate that you know that context is an important aspect in understanding the play. You will have to comment on why the context is significant rather than simply giving examples of what the context was.

Context can be understood in more than one way. It can refer to:

- the context of the characters who feature in the play
- the context of the audience of the play at the time it was first published/performed
- the context of the present-day audience.

In your assessment, you may have to reflect on all three levels of context as part of your response.

City life

Nowadays, approximately 54% of the UK population lives in a city. The southeast of England, where Christopher and his family live, is the most populous area in the country and continues to expand. House prices are highest in this area. Employment opportunities are plentiful but many of the jobs available are unskilled and low paid.

For autistic Christopher and his struggling parents, the proximity of so many other people has an impact on the way they live and the jobs they do. Ed appears to be a self-employed plumber. Though being his own boss enables Ed to choose where and when he works, it also puts pressure on him as he is now the sole breadwinner (only person earning money) to support the home and Christopher. Ed has to make choices about going to work, which involves leaving Christopher alone: **'I've just had a call there's a lady. Her cellar has flooded. I've got to go out and fix it'** *(Part One)*. The audience learns that he has virtually no one else now on whom he can call for support if Christopher has a problem. The neighbours appear only when Christopher is investigating Wellington's death. There is no evidence that they are known well. This is a facet of modern city living that Stephens exemplifies – many people have no relationship with those who live nearest to them. This may be a choice that Ed has made due to Christopher's difficulties with 'strangers' so that there are fewer opportunities for problems.

When Christopher decides to leave home, he has to contend with problems he has never come across, namely dealing with the busyness of people, roads, transport and noise. Stephens initially shows how he is confused and overwhelmed by what he is facing to reach Judy, but how quickly he starts to apply his knowledge to solve the problem: **'... if something is nearby you can find it by moving in a spiral, walking clockwise and taking every right turn'** *(Part Two)*. By using the Voices at the railway stations, Stephens recreates the sensation Christopher

CONTEXT

has of being unable to 'phase out' some of the noise so he can work out what to do to get to London and then Willesden. The unfamiliar setting and the challenge of travelling alone are emphasized by this disturbing mix of sounds, which the audience also hears.

Another example of Christopher's ignorance of life in London is shown in the scene in the tube when he follows the escaped Toby onto the rail line, much to the consternation of other people: **'I can't get back up there I need to get my rat'** *(Part Two)*. Never having used the tube, Christopher is unaware of the law about going onto the line or the very real danger that he might be killed. The risk is only obvious to the onlookers and audience.

It's not surprising that Christopher experiences sensory overload on his travels through London

Stephens also shows how Christopher does not understand the unwritten social code that on the tube no one speaks to each other! Christopher tries to find out if he has been bundled onto the right train but no one responds to his question, **'Is this train going to Willesden Junction?'** *(Part Two)*. He has to rely on the automatic announcements to know when to get off. Though he shuns human contact, Christopher is unused to being ignored when he asks a question and this also adds to the sense of disorientation that Stephens creates.

Being in a city like London can be frightening for a person without autism. Stephens shows the impact that the city has on Christopher when he is seen wandering the streets in the early hours of the morning. Christopher again applies his knowledge of science to help him deal with the sense of confusion: **'All the light from the streetlights and car headlights and floodlights… reflect off tiny particles in the atmosphere…'** *(Part Two)*. When Judy finds him in the street, she is worried about him leaving the flat alone and the people he might meet while out. She does not seem surprised that he has gone into the street in the early hours; she is only concerned for his safety there. This implies that she was less worried about his night-time wandering in Swindon, perhaps because there were fewer people there.

In the concluding remarks about his adventure, Christopher comments that **'I don't like London and there are universities in lots of places and not all of them are in big cities'** *(Part Two)*. His brief experience of city life is enough for him to know that he would not choose to live in a city when he becomes an adult. Stephens shows that the city makes Christopher more fearful while he is there but, once he has been able to return home, proud that he managed to navigate through it. City life, for that brief period, has contributed to his increased independence and maturity.

Activity 4

Stephens portrays the city through dialogue and movement. Focus on the ways that different people in London speak to Christopher. Choose three characters who interact with him on his journey and write about how Stephens shows the differing attitudes of these strangers to the autistic teenager.

Literary context

The account of Christopher and his investigation into Wellington's death began life as a novel. Mark Haddon, the author, had an immediate success with the novel and was approached with the idea of turning it into a play almost from the start. He rejected those ideas for quite a long time because he had serious doubts that the novel, which is set mainly in the mind of Christopher and so has a first-person narrator, could be adapted into a different medium without compromising the story.

In the end, Haddon decided to approach a respected playwright himself rather than waiting for someone else to tackle it. He chose to work with playwright Simon Stephens and the director Marianne Elliott.

This transfer from the page to the stage is not an uncommon one. Many popular films and TV programmes begin life as a novel or short story. The success of a novel often encourages film-makers and playwrights to think about how that powerful story can be shown to a wider audience. However, a successful novel does not necessarily mean the film or play version will be equally successful, and this is another factor that Haddon was concerned about. He expressed the desire that '… they would use the novel to create a great piece of theatre, and second, more selfishly, that they would make *Curious Incident* new again'. Haddon felt that all the questions he had answered and all the interviews he had done about the novel had only served to make him feel distant from it and unsure of his reasons for writing it in the first place. The success of the play came about, he felt, because the audience could see how other characters reacted to Christopher and the events, which was not shown in the novel. He felt that the play added new dimensions to his original story and made the audience think more carefully about themselves. He concluded: 'It is never simply a story acted, just as the novel is never simply a story told'.

Activity 5

Think about Mark Haddon's comment: 'It is never simply a story acted'. Explain what you think he meant by that. What do you think the play shows about people living in the early part of the 21st century?

CONTEXT

Upgrade

Writing about context

In your assessment you may be expected to show your understanding of the ways in which context is revealed by Stephens. For example, a response to a question dealing with isolation of the characters might include the following points:

> Stephens shows that each of the main characters appears to live **an isolated life, as each one has only one other person with whom they seem to interact in a meaningful way.** Since Judy left, Ed has tried to build a relationship with Mrs Shears: **'I thought she might want to move in here.'** But this failed, leaving him to deal with **the isolation of being a single parent** and lacking any emotional support himself. This reflects the fact that **many people living in cities are cut off from close family because they need to work.** Coping with **bringing up a disabled child is also an isolating factor** as Ed shows when he has to deal on his own with all the difficulties that creates. This is seen especially when he confronts Judy about her long absence from their lives, **creating sympathy in the audience.**

- Comments on the key topic with a specific example.
- Includes a supporting quotation to emphasize the point.
- Refers to a social issue.
- Extends the contextual reference with more detailed explanation.
- Focuses on the key topic with an additional point.
- Shows the response of a modern audience.

Characters

Main characters

Christopher

Christopher is the narrator and main character of the play, but during the course of it he is shown to be an **imperfect narrator**. He chooses which parts to share with the audience and which conversations to recount. He describes himself in very precise terms: *'My name is Christopher John Francis Boone. I know all the countries of the world and the capital cities'* (Part One). This is probably not the way the majority of 15-year-olds would introduce themselves. It reflects the way that Christopher's mind works and flags up from early in the play that his thinking patterns will be uncommon.

Though never stated in the play, it might be assumed that Christopher has the form of autism called Asperger syndrome. His own perspective is flawed because of his autism, so the audience is presented with the story from a restricted view. He can recall details that other people would dismiss, he observes things in greater detail than most people and is seen to have a good memory: *'Come on you're the memory man…'* (Part One). Other characters are used to voice what he remembers them saying at other times or in other places. His life prospects appear to be limited because of his autistic difficulties.

Throughout the play, Christopher's interests show themselves through his dialogue and his absolute focus on what he knows or can deduce from evidence. He is most interested in maths, astronomy, science and technology. He refers to these frequently: *'Some people think the Milky Way is a long line of stars, but it isn't. Our galaxy is a huge disc of stars…'* (Part One). These subjects represent his need for stability and predictability, and are all based on reason, facts and logic.

Christopher dislikes things that have unknown or unpredictable outcomes. He shares with Siobhan that *'I don't always do what I'm told… Because… it is usually confusing and does not make sense'* (Part One). He finds it difficult to understand something that does not appear to be logical, so disregards it. This has consequences when his father

Christopher often struggles to make sense of things and this is reflected in the stage production

imperfect narrator a narrator who tells events from a single point of view

tells him to stop investigating Wellington's death as he does not think the instruction makes sense. He wants to solve the mystery and does not understand why Ed does not share this view. He is upset by Wellington's death as it is unexpected and unexplained. He needs to find out who is responsible in order to find a resolution to the problem. He is the only character to think this. No other character appears to have the same need, again indicating that Christopher is unusual.

> **Activity 1**
>
> Select three details about Christopher that indicate to you that he is an unusual 15-year-old. Write a paragraph about each detail, supported by at least one quotation, explaining why he does not conform to society's expectations of teenagers.

Christopher is the only teenager in the play. The other characters are all adults. Christopher appears to have no friends. He knows other students at school but they are not like him. Other students seem to have more profound difficulties than Christopher: **'Steve… who comes to school on Thursdays needs help eating his food'** *(Part One)*. However, Christopher does not appear to worry about this. His understanding of human relationships is limited to knowing about them. He cannot cope with being touched by anyone, even his parents. He does not understand emotions and so reacts in an extreme way when his father admits to killing the dog in a fit of temper. He categorizes people who are safe as **'… a friend or a member of my family'** *(Part One)*. He does not distinguish between the importance of people and the importance of animals. To him, they are equal, hence his extreme reaction to Ed's admission and his subsequent fear for his own safety.

During the night, Christopher is seen to be wandering the streets of London. Ed also refers to this, which suggests to the audience that it may be a recurrent problem. Christopher was in Mrs Shears's garden after midnight when he found the dead Wellington. He walks around London and converses with Siobhan in his head about his anxiety and fear of Mr Shears. Even this is an opportunity for him to think about the science he knows, but now he also links it to the life lessons he is learning: **'… if you have difficult things in your life it is nice to think that they are what is called negligible which means they are so small you don't have to take them into account'** *(Part Two)*.

Christopher develops and changes significantly as the play progresses. Stephens shows how the teenager uses his interests and sense of right and wrong to make a journey that is literal (to London to find his mother) and metaphorical (to push the boundaries of what he thought he could do in order to achieve his purpose). By the end of the play, Christopher has matured because he is learning how relationships can adapt and change as well as discovering that his dreams of working in science could be achievable.

CHARACTERS

Although the main character in the play, Christopher may also be regarded as a **metaphor**. He may represent the way that many people dislike and fear change and difference. His journey to discover a new place and learn about others is seen as painful and difficult, but not impossible: **'… it will be difficult at first because… because it's a difficult project. But it will get better'** *(Part Two)*. The audience sees Christopher overcoming profound disability to achieve his goal and is forced to confront their own fears about stepping out of their comfort zone to deal with issues that arise in the course of living.

> **metaphor** a comparison of one thing to another to make a description more vivid; a metaphor states that one thing *is* the other

Activity 2

Through the character of Christopher, what does the play teach you about taking on challenges and overcoming difficulties?

a) Identify three key points in the play when Christopher tackles a challenge or difficulty. Explore how he approaches each one.

b) Suggest what lessons could be learned from this by the audience.

Tips for assessment

Upgrade

For the exam, you will need to be able to write about the main character(s) from the text in detail. It will be useful to have a clear idea about the ways in which they develop and change at key moments. Create a flow chart for each main character, linking the events that are seen with the development of attributes of each character. This may also be useful as a visual way to remind yourself of the sequence of events.

Ed

Ed is Christopher's father and the person he lives with at the beginning of the play. As a single father, Ed is trying to make sure that he can work to provide a secure financial basis for them both and also trying to provide the emotional support Christopher needs: **'Christopher you have to stay out of trouble, OK?'** *(Part One)*.

It is clear from their interactions in the first scene, after Christopher has been arrested, that their relationship can be volatile. Ed loses patience quite quickly when he is trying to impress on Christopher that he should not investigate Wellington's death. This gives the audience the impression that it may be the type of conversation that has occurred before, about other issues. Ed struggles to make sure that Christopher complies. This appears to be a typical relationship between a father and a teenage son. Ed, as father, wants to be in control of what Christopher does; Christopher, probably trying to deal with unfamiliar hormones, wants to start making his own choices.

Ed and Christopher communicate in a form of shorthand, which shows the audience how close their bond can be: **'He holds his hand out in front of him with his fingers stretched. Christopher does the same. They touch fingers. Then let go'** *(Part One)*. The physical contact between them is limited to this simple touch but is enough to show the level of understanding that exists between them. Christopher has issues with being touched so this finger contact is all he can manage. However, on occasion, their interactions become aggressive as Ed tries to make Christopher comply with his expectations. He hits Christopher when he becomes frustrated with him and angry about his apparent lack of honesty about talking to Mrs Alexander: **'Ed grabs Christopher's arm. Christopher screams. They fight each other'** *(Part One)*. The audience is shocked by the ferocity of the characters' responses. Afterwards, Ed justifies his actions by blaming them on worry about what Christopher might get himself into. This foreshadows the later revelation that Ed killed Wellington in a fit of temper and forms part of the reason why Christopher feels unsafe with him.

Although there is a close bond between Christopher and his father, they touch only with fingertips

CHARACTERS

> **Activity 3**
>
> Do you think Ed is a good or a bad father? Refer to three points in the play to support your views and write a paragraph about each example you have chosen. Share your views with a partner.

The revelation that Ed has lied for two years about the whereabouts of Christopher's mother comes as a shock to the audience as well as to Christopher. In addition to this, he has also concealed her letters to prevent Christopher from finding out the truth. He was unable to explain to his son what really happened to his mother, perhaps due to his own hurt and anger: **'… because I didn't know how to explain it was so complicated… It got out of control'** *(Part One)*. Ed is not a deliberately cruel father. However, the audience is left with the impression that he struggled to cope with his wife's betrayal and, due to Christopher's disability, he could not find a way to account for her absence to their son.

Their relationship is completely shattered by the revelation that Ed killed the dog. This outcome of Ed's temper and unpredictable reactions triggers Christopher's investigation and is what causes him to run away from his father. It is at this point that the audience becomes aware of the **irony** of what Ed has done.

Towards the end of the play, Ed shows his love for Christopher as he tries to rebuild the relationship. He shows his understanding of what Christopher needs in the way he addresses the problems they both face: **'… let's call it a project. A project we have to do together… I have to show you that you can trust me'** *(Part Two)*. Ed has planned a way forward and buying a puppy affirms his good intentions. The dog has the double role of showing that Ed knows his son's concerns, and also provides protective reassurance for the very fears that Christopher has expressed. By the end of the play, the audience sees that Ed and Christopher are moving towards a better relationship and so they will eventually become a stronger family than they were previously.

Ed, like Christopher, is seen to be a flawed character. He is presented as an imperfect father who is unsure how to deal with the problems caused by family breakdown and his son's difficulties. His solutions to his problems are also imperfect. He could be seen to represent many parents who are trying to work out how best to deal with their increasingly independent teenage children.

> **irony** the difference between what a character would be expected to do and what they actually do, often for comic effect

CHARACTERS

> **Activity 4**
>
> Look again at Ed's final speeches to Christopher and the accompanying stage directions from **'Christopher, can I have a talk with you?'** *(Part Two)*. Then answer the following questions.
>
> - What does this section show about Ed's hopes for the future with Christopher?
> - How does it reveal how well he knows his son?
> - Why do you think Stephens chose this way for Ed to finish his role in the play?

Judy

Judy is Christopher's mother. From early in the play, the audience believes that she is dead and does not discover until later that this is not true but made up by Ed to try and protect Christopher. In fact, she left the family home to live with her new partner Roger Shears. Initially, the only things the audience learns about her are through Christopher's memories and then through her letters to him.

Hints about Judy's life are delivered by Mrs Alexander, who seems to feel that Christopher should know the truth. The revelations about his mother are interspersed with memories drawn out by Siobhan. The audience receives this information in a piecemeal fashion and they assemble the truth gradually. This reflects the way in which Christopher's mind works when he has to deal with complicated ideas – he has to put the different pieces together over a period of time until he can understand the whole idea.

Christopher recounts his memory of holidaying with Judy when he was nine. She is seen as someone who was fun and who tries to encourage Christopher to enjoy things too. Her prank when she dives underwater is completely misunderstood by Christopher, who cannot comprehend where she might be. He thinks she has been eaten by a shark. The shock of her disappearance causes him to scream. It may be the memory of this that makes Judy disappear with Roger Shears without telling her son.

In the memory, Judy is portrayed as a woman who has dreams beyond her current situation. She speaks frankly and openly about her desire to live a more exciting and 'romantic' life. This suggests that her marriage has not fulfilled her expectations and that being a mother has created greater problems than she is capable of dealing with: **'If I hadn't married your father I think I'd be living in a little farmhouse in the South of France with someone called Jean'** *(Part One)*. Her dream would have meant that Christopher would not have been born, but this does not appear to occur to her. The inappropriateness of this discussion with her nine-year-old son also does not appear to cross her mind. The audience might therefore form the impression that Judy is unreliable.

CHARACTERS

> ### Activity 5
>
> Look at the description in Part One, Episode 8 of the Cornwall holiday. Focus on Judy's memories of it.
>
> **a)** Draw five images, one for each section of the memory. Pick out a detail you feel best shows what Judy is like as a mother.
>
> **b)** Write a sentence explaining each image and why you chose it. Compare your ideas with those of a partner.

When Christopher starts to read Judy's letters, the audience learns for the first time that she is not dead. The letters also allow the audience to learn about the difficult life Judy felt she had while trying to look after her son. For example, she says that during a Christmas shopping trip **'… you wouldn't let me touch you and you just lay on the floor and screamed'** *(Part One)*. The examples she gives of situations when she lost control of events show her difficulties in bringing up her autistic son. He was not easy to manage and at times was given to unpredictable, aggressive behaviour. The audience sees that she became less confident in her abilities as a mother because she found Christopher so hard to deal with, whereas she saw Ed being able to remain calm.

Judy implies that she was also suffering with a form of depression: **'I just cried and cried and cried…'** *(Part One)*. She seems to have justified her choice to go with Roger as being in Christopher's best interests. By the end of hearing her letters, the audience hears again about her dreams – **'I used to have dreams that everything would get better'** *(Part One)* – but realizes that they were just as unrealistic as her expectations of Christopher.

Judy's expectations over the intervening two years seem unaltered when she encounters Christopher outside her flat. She has not seen him in all that time and her first instinct is to hug him, which provokes his usual response because he does not like being touched: **'She goes to hug him. He pushes her away so hard that he falls over'** *(Part Two)*. This initial encounter perhaps shows that things are not going to work out as either of them expects or wants. She has no hesitation in telling Christopher that he can stay as long as he wants. However, it is Roger who introduces the practical difficulties: **'What's he going to do? There's no school for him to go to. We've both got jobs. It's bloody ridiculous'** *(Part Two)*. This is another example of the way Judy clings on to her unrealistic idea of what her family 'should' be like, without considering the consequences.

Judy also does not understand the importance of the A level exam to Christopher. She has had no contact with him for a long time and he has altered more than she realizes. Her reaction to him travelling to London by train shows that she imagined his life would be more limited, as does her response when he explains about the exam: **'I can ring the school. We can get it postponed. You can take it some other time'** *(Part Two)*. Christopher knows that is not possible, indicating his increasing maturity as he moves towards a future he has planned for himself. Ignoring him, Judy informs the school that Christopher will not take the exam. Once he knows, Christopher screams until hoarse and then adopts a form of hunger strike. Judy is unable to break through his silence and resistance but, when Roger assaults her son while drunk, realizes that her only option is to take him back to Swindon.

By the end of the play, the audience sees Judy and Christopher learning how to live together in a setting neither finds easy. Both are having to compromise. Each of them is building a life that includes Ed again. Judy appears to have put aside her dreams in order to concentrate on the reality of bringing up her son in a way that meets his needs. Her final words in the play reveal that she is committed to him: **'We'll come back tomorrow and you can see him then'** *(Part Two)*. At this point, the audience respects her more as they have been allowed to see the internal and external difficulties that forced her to leave Christopher in the first place. Like him, she has also matured and learned to accept the world as it really is.

Activity 6

How does Stephens present Judy as a character that changes during the play? Refer to key points in the play that show the changes she undergoes.

Tips for assessment

Upgrade

When a question asks you to write about a character, it is important to remember that the character was created by Stephens for a specific purpose. Each character represents a different feature of the 'message' Stephens wants to give the audience. Think about:

- how Stephens has chosen to present that character to affect audience response
- why Stephens chose to present the character in that way
- what purpose the character has in the whole play.

Minor characters

Siobhan

Siobhan has a dual role. She is a character in the story because she is Christopher's teacher at school but she is also the narrator who voices Christopher's thoughts, as recorded in his book. At some points, she is involved in discussion with Christopher about aspects of his life. At other points, she appears as a 'critical friend', reading his book about the investigation into Wellington's death.

In some ways Siobhan appears to be a substitute for Christopher's mother. She clearly cares about him because she encourages him, supports his ambitions and

CHARACTERS

shows interest in what he is doing: **'This is good Christopher. It's quite exciting. I like the details'** *(Part One).* She enables him to use his imagination and intellect, so could also be regarded as a good teacher. It is clear that Christopher trusts her as he confides in her and shares his dreams about his future with her.

Siobhan reacts to what Christopher says and does so more honestly than either of his parents. She is present when he decides to continue investigating Wellington's death, although she also reinforces what Ed has said: **'I think you should do what your father tells you to do'** *(Part One).* She is the first person to hear about his A level result and the person he asks to confirm that he can now do anything. She is the consistent adult in his life as both his parents are seen to be unstable in different ways.

Siobhan could be considered as a main character as she features in a lot of the action in the play. However, she shows very little development during the course of the play and her role is mainly in reaction to Christopher. She is not observed to have a life of her own. It is referred to, but never seen. For example, Christopher twice refers to living at her house when he is uncomfortable about his current living arrangements. In both cases, Siobhan refuses to accept his idea and refers him back to his parents. Her role begins and ends at the school gates.

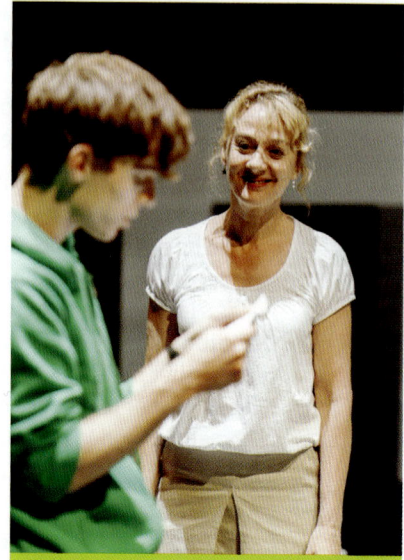

Siobhan encourages Christopher in his ambitions and is the first to learn of his exam result

Activity 7

Look at the ways in which Siobhan and Christopher interact. Write answers to the questions below.

- Why do you think Siobhan is needed as a character?
- What does her character help to show the audience about Christopher that would not be possible otherwise?
- Does her character change in the way that other characters are seen to change? Explain your answer by referring to particular points in the play.

Mrs Alexander

Although Mrs Alexander claims to be Christopher's 'friend', she is the catalyst for him leaving home to find his mother. The audience sees her more as a well-disposed busybody. She offers Christopher a drink and biscuits when he is investigating Wellington's death and then later tells him the truth about the relationship between his mother and Mr Shears.

Her relationship with Christopher develops to a point where he is willing to entrust Toby to Mrs Alexander when he is leaving home, but it does not advance beyond that point because **'I can't stay overnight in your house or use your toilet because you've used it and you're a stranger'** *(Part One)*. Mrs Alexander tries to help Christopher by looking for common ground with him. She mentions her own grandson being a similar age, the fact that she sees Christopher going to school on the bus and she shows interest in Toby, but to no avail. Christopher still considers her to be outside the group of people he thinks of as family friends.

Mr Shears

Despite being Judy's new partner, Roger Shears is not presented very sympathetically. He seems to be unaware that Christopher has autism and so has no appreciation of the difficulties the teenager has faced in reaching his mother. Roger is more interested in how his own life may be disrupted by Christopher's arrival: **'This flat is hardly big enough for two people, let alone three'** *(Part Two)*. He is seen to be quite aggressive towards both Christopher and Ed. However, he tries to calm the situation between Judy and Ed to prevent them rowing, which is totally ignored by them both, perhaps suggesting that he is not particularly significant to either of them.

Roger fetches Christopher some library books, but misjudges their suitability so they are dismissed by Christopher: **'They're for children. They're not very good'** *(Part Two)*. He does not take time to get to know Christopher as an individual so makes inappropriate choices without consulting him. This reflects the way society often judges people with any form of disability, regardless of their actual capability. Disabled people often complain about this sort of treatment.

Roger's relationship with Judy seems to be destabilized following Christopher's arrival, suggesting that he also struggles to adjust to change. He points out the difficulties of trying to accommodate Christopher with them but his tone and word choice make his quite reasonable comments seem hostile. After he has got drunk and assaulted Christopher, Judy leaves him and he is not seen in the play again.

Mr Shears's name seems to be ironic. Gardening shears are used to cut down plants and grass. In the play, Roger is responsible for inducing Judy to leave her family, effectively cutting her off from Christopher.

Activity 8

Ed comments to Christopher about Roger Shears, **'That man is evil'** *(Part One)*.

a) What evidence can you find from Roger's actions and speech that supports this assessment of his personality?

b) Why do you think Ed believes it to be true?

CHARACTERS

Mrs Shears

When the play opens, Mrs Shears expresses shock at finding Wellington dead. She repeats herself several times – *'Get away from my dog' (Part One)*, emphasizing that she is lost for words. She is quick to jump to the conclusion that Christopher is to blame because he is there in the garden too. She calls the police.

Later, when Christopher is trying to find out who killed her dog, she reacts to him with hostility, clearly believing he was responsible. She may represent the view that, due to his disability, Christopher is unable to control his behaviour and in her eyes that makes him a suspect for the killing.

At some point before the start of the play, Mrs Shears was regarded by Christopher as a family friend. Ed clearly implies that his relationship with Mrs Shears was once based on more than friendship. However, it did not last, which was part of the reason he ended up killing her dog: *'Mrs Shears… she was very good to me… I thought she might carry on coming over… I thought she might… eventually… want to move in here' (Part One)*. Ed explains this to Christopher, who does not respond or ask questions so the audience is left to guess the circumstances around the developing friendship and what Mrs Shears might have said to Ed to bring it to an end.

Mrs Gascoyne

Mrs Gascoyne is the headteacher at Christopher's school. Despite being in charge of the school, she is presented as not understanding Christopher and his needs. She tries to leave Christopher out of discussions about his exam prospects: *'We should talk about this later. Maybe on our own' (Part One)*. This attitude goes against advice on improving opportunities for young people with disabilities and it seems strange to the audience that Christopher, who is very good at explaining his hopes for the future, might be excluded from making decisions that will affect him.

Mrs Gascoyne appears to be unaware of Christopher's exceptional ability at maths. She confuses the idea of providing a personalized education with treating all students the same. She could be regarded as representing the inflexible nature of education, whether in mainstream or special school, and the view that any student should only do what every other student does. This is ironic because she manages a special school, which theoretically exists to meet the individual needs of students who cannot cope with mainstream school.

Mrs Gascoyne's limited view of Christopher seems to be reflected in the way she is presented by Stephens. With the exception of the scene described above, she appears to say only what has already been said by other characters and she never speaks to Christopher directly.

Reverend Peters

As a vicar, Reverend Peters is presented in a way that suggests he is not very knowledgeable about his own faith or able to deal with questions about the relationship between science and Christianity. He is first seen very briefly when

Christopher asks where heaven is located. His answer does not conform to Christopher's knowledge about the construction of the universe, so Peters finds he is being challenged on theology (the study of God) by a 15-year-old boy with a better knowledge of science than his own. His response suggests a lack of confidence in dealing with the challenge: **'... we should talk about this on another day when I have more time'** *(Part One)*. At this point, Peters seems to represent the difficulties the Church has in reconciling faith in God with scientific knowledge.

Reverend Peters appears to be a governor at the school and a trusted person who can be called upon to help in various situations. Later in the play, Peters invigilates Christopher's exam. In this role, he is supportive and encouraging, although he will not bend the rules to help Christopher when he can't read the questions: **'... I'm afraid I can't help you like that. I'm not allowed to'** *(Part Two)*. He is involved in Christopher's education only to help him take the exam and there is no suggestion that he ever follows up the conversation about the location of heaven.

Activity 9

Reverend Peters appears only briefly in the play during two episodes. In what ways does he contribute to the audience's better understanding of Christopher? Look at the interactions between the two characters, then write a paragraph about each scene to answer the question.

Policemen

A number of different policemen are involved at various points during the play. They each represent the importance of the law and the issues that sometimes occur in trying to make sure that laws are applied consistently. They all appear to be unaware of the difficulties Christopher is struggling with. This suggests the perception that his disability is largely 'invisible' because he looks as if he should be able to cope with everyday situations without much support.

Policeman One

This policeman, called after the death of Wellington, questions Christopher about his involvement in the dog's death, seeming to assume that the teenager knows more than he says, perhaps suggesting that he expects teenage boys to be economical with the truth: **'You seem very upset about this. I'm going to ask you once again'** *(Part One)*.

The policeman tries to lift Christopher from the ground when he doesn't stop groaning. Both characters are shocked by the violent reaction that provokes, and so is the audience. For the first time, this episode shows that Christopher's disability prevents him from managing his emotions in socially acceptable ways. The language the policeman uses shows him moving from a professional to a personal response: **'... if you try any of that monkey business again you little shit...'** *(Part One)*. This shocks the audience because police officers are expected to be professional even when provoked. This is perhaps meant to show that Christopher's difficulties challenge even professionals, and foreshadows the struggles his parents have in bringing him up.

Duty Sergeant

This character is the one who takes Christopher into custody after his arrest. He asks Christopher to complete a series of tasks, which seem to be standard ones when someone is arrested: **'Could you empty your pocket onto the desk please?'** *(Part One)*. However, Christopher refuses to remove his watch and then screams when the Duty Sergeant attempts to take it. The Duty Sergeant stops at once. This perhaps shows that he has greater experience as a senior officer and realizes that Christopher cannot be treated in the same way as other people.

His compassion and humour are seen when he interviews Christopher: **'Right. Lovely. Do you know your father's phone number Christopher?'** *(Part One)*. He appears to realize that Christopher is not going to give him standard responses to questions so takes care to explain what things mean. When he questions Christopher later, with Ed, he makes his questions very clear. He shows patience in dealing with the situation although the responses he gets seem unusual.

The Duty Sergeant is perhaps meant to show that the authorities are not insensitive to the difficulties people experience but are not always sure how to deal with them.

Station Policeman

In Part Two, the Station Policeman tries to help Christopher but also finds that conversation is difficult because of the literal way Christopher interprets the questions: **'OK let's keep it simple. What are you doing at the railway station?'** Their initial conversation is positive in tone and the Station Policeman appears to be supportive when Christopher is confused about what to do or where to go. This alters, however, when he discovers that Christopher has run away but refuses to go to the police station. The tone of their conversation becomes more hostile: **'Now listen, you little monkey. You can either do what I say, or I'm going to have to make…'** *(Part Two)*. The Station Policeman's mood becomes worse when the train sets off and he is trapped on board. This is reflected in his language as he swears about the situation and loses patience with Christopher. The interactions between them are brought to an abrupt end when Christopher hides in the luggage rack. The policeman continues to search but fails to spot where he has hidden.

The Station Policeman makes Christopher anxious because of the authority he represents, but the teenager does not want to obey him. This produces conflict in Christopher because he does not like lies and disobedience. This could show that Christopher is beginning to grow up and deal with conflicting feelings about authority figures.

London Policeman

The policeman in London arrives at the flat in response to Ed reporting that Christopher has run away. He appears to be the only policeman who takes Christopher at his word. He questions him directly to check facts and, when Christopher says he wants to stay with his mother, he does not pursue the matter any further. He is dealing only with the issue of Christopher going missing and makes it clear that the family needs to sort out its domestic issues without help from the law: '**... you're going to have to sort this out among yourselves**' *(Part Two)*. He reappears briefly when Ed arrives at the flat and then gets Ed to leave instead of rowing with Judy.

Activity 10

Look at the conversations between the police officers and Christopher. Then answer the questions below.

- How do the answers given to the questions show that Christopher does not fully understand the gravity of the situations?
- How does the writer show the humour in the conversations?

Members of the public

Most members of the public in the play do not interact with Christopher unless he does or says something to attract their attention. When he does speak to them, their responses mirror the ways people treat those they do not understand or are unsure how to deal with. Their attitudes could be regarded as **stereotypical** of how disabled people are regarded and treated by society.

stereotypical reflecting a fixed idea of what someone or something is, developed through seeing it in this way over a period of time

Wellington

Although Wellington only appears after his death, he is the trigger for the events that the play deals with. Christopher, who believes animals are as important as humans, does not understand why the police will not be investigating Wellington's 'murder' in the same way they would investigate a human's murder. It is for this reason that he begins to investigate it himself.

Wellington's death at the beginning of the play could perhaps be seen as a metaphor for the end of Christopher's childhood and the beginning of his adulthood as he learns to deal with difficult situations and topics.

Language

The language used in the play is a factor in its success. Throughout the play, Stephens has chosen words that are intended to impact on the audience. You will be expected to show that you can explore the impact of the language and how the word choices reveal aspects of the characters or **themes**.

When interviewed about the way that the novel was turned into a play, Stephens said that he focused first on the dialogue written by Mark Haddon. He used this as the basis for the drama so that there are clear links and similarities between the two formats of the story.

Realistic tone

Stephens adopts language that seems realistic to the audience. The dialogue appears to be very similar to the type of conversation that might be heard in many households with teenagers: **'I have just had a phone call from Mrs Shears. What the hell were you doing poking round her garden?'** *(Part One)*. The characters use a range of language conventions in the dialogue, which makes their speech sound realistic, including questioning, repetition, **ellipsis** and a mix of short and long sentences. This realistic dialogue helps the audience to believe in what Stephens is depicting and very easily become absorbed in the unfolding drama. It also gives the feeling that the events are fresh and current, so the situations still seem relevant.

Although Stephens makes the dialogue sound like real conversation, it is important to remember that its purpose is to move the story on and allow the audience to understand the characters better. Part of Stephens's skill is to make the speech sound like casual remarks.

> **ellipsis** an omission of words
>
> **theme** a subject or idea that is repeated or developed in a literary work

Activity 1

Look at the conversation in Part One from **'Where have you been?'** to **'... a Dream Come True'**.

- In what ways does Stephens make this appear to be a conventional row between a parent and a teenager?
- How does the conversation introduce new aspects to the storyline?
- How does it reveal different aspects of the characters of Ed and Christopher?

Swearing

From the outset, swearing is a feature of the language used by most of the characters, e.g. **'What in fuck's name have you done to my dog?'** *(Part One)*. The impact of this opening is to create both shock and amusement in the audience. This type of

LANGUAGE

language is continued throughout the play by most characters except Christopher, Siobhan and Mrs Alexander. However, Stephens does not use this language without good reason. He chooses it to ensure that the audience understands the characters' emotions and shares the sense of shock or alarm being portrayed. Much of the swearing appears to be directed at Christopher or used about him, e.g. **'… you little shit'** *(Part One)*, **'It's a bloody dog Christopher'** *(Part One)*, **'You are a bloody handful…'** *(Part Two)*. It serves to emphasize the frustration many characters experience when trying to sort out an issue caused by Christopher's disability.

Christopher does not swear and he questions the language used by other characters – **'Why are you swearing?'** *(Part Two)* – which implies that he understands the words but does not understand the emotions that cause someone to swear. This shows that Christopher's inability to relate to feelings also extends to an inability to express himself.

Siobhan is only seen in relation to Christopher, in her role as his teacher. As a role model to young people, she would not swear during her working day. It would also be inappropriate for Stephens to allow her to swear because that would undermine the formal and professional tone of her conversations with Christopher. The formal way she speaks enables Christopher to respond appropriately. She does not cause him to become stressed through what she says, which is different to how other characters affect him. She speaks in a non-threatening way. She asks him a number of questions intended to help him clarify things, e.g. **'What was your mother like Christopher? Do you remember much about her?'** *(Part One)*. To some extent these are **rhetorical questions**, as Christopher can choose not to answer them, but they help him reveal more of his thoughts, which he may not volunteer otherwise. Siobhan also uses repetition throughout the play, to reinforce ideas she wants Christopher to understand. Stephens makes her language clear and echo the way Christopher speaks so he is confident when talking to her.

Mrs Alexander is the oldest character with whom Christopher interacts. Stephens has not included swearing as part of her dialogue, which possibly reflects the fact that many older people think swearing is unacceptable. Her use of swearing would not seem natural for a friendly older lady.

As well as the use of conventional swear words, Stephens also includes **expletives** based on

Christopher and Ed voice their frustration with each other

expletive a swear word

rhetorical question a question asked to create a dramatic effect or to make a point

religion. This used to be referred to as 'taking the Lord's name in vain', meaning using one of the names of God to emphasize frustration or impatience, e.g. **'Oh Christ, you've wet yourself'** *(Part Two)*.

> **Activity 2**
>
> **a)** Think about the way swearing is used in the play.
> - What response from the audience do you think Stephens was aiming for when he chose to use it?
> - Does the swearing have more than one purpose in the play?
>
> **b)** Write a paragraph in response to each question.

Humour

It is ironic that Christopher claims to have no sense of humour because the play has quite a few funny moments. Many of these occur because of Stephens's language choices. The adult characters make jokes that are understood by the audience but not by Christopher. Much of this humour is based on sarcasm as the adults respond to Christopher's questions, for example, when the shopkeeper replies **'No it's a sodding crocodile'** *(Part Two)*.

Christopher responds by simply repeating the question because the answer does not make sense to him, so the Shopkeeper is forced to answer him properly. Here humour is created by juxtaposing the obvious in the question with the ridiculousness of the initial response.

Humour also comes from the reactions of other characters to what Christopher says in his very straightforward way, e.g. the exchange in Part One about Battenberg cake. Christopher's description uses mathematical terms like 'square' and 'equally', but is completely correct. It is the contrast between Mrs Alexander's startled responses and Christopher's **deadpan** answers that creates amusement. Another example is created during the scene when Toby escapes on the underground. The street language of the Punk Girl – **'Help him den, you muppet'** *(Part Two)* – is in sharp contrast to the matter-of-fact Christopher. Stephens captures her **accent** by using **phonetic spelling**. The way she speaks to the Man with Socks brings out the comedy as well as the tension in the situation.

> **accent** the way someone pronounces words in a language
> **deadpan** lacking in expression; saying something amusing in a serious manner
> **phonetic spelling** words spelt using letters that express the exact sounds

LANGUAGE

> **Activity 3**
>
> Look through the play again. Pick out two places where you feel humour is shown through sarcasm, juxtaposition, adult responses or specific language choice. Explain how Stephens uses language in each of these instances to create comedy.

Christopher's language

Stephens has made Christopher speak quite differently to any of the other characters. This is partly to reflect the fact that he is different in his way of thinking and behaving but also to give the audience a better understanding of the way his mind works. Christopher's speeches reveal his thought processes and this enables us to both empathize with him and yet notice that he is different.

The language Stephens has given Christopher appears to be very precise. He often refers to facts and things that can be proved, e.g. **'After twelve and a half minutes...'** *(Part One)*, **'He killed a dog. With a garden fork...'** *(Part Two)*. Stephens has made Christopher provide details about events and circumstances almost to the point of being pedantic (overly concerned with small details or rules). It is a trait that the audience immediately finds to be unusual but gradually comes to realize reflects the way Christopher thinks.

The way Christopher speaks reveals that he has an almost photographic recall of events, even if they are quite distant in time or appear insignificant to others, e.g. **'I remember 20 July 2006. I was 9 years old. It was a Saturday...'** *(Part One)*. The short sentences make Christopher's statements sound believable and make the audience trust him. He says himself that he does not tell lies and he speaks in such a way that the audience is convinced this is true.

Christopher's language also reveals his intelligence. He can explain complex ideas clearly in such a way that the audience understands what he is saying, e.g. **'... the gravity of a black hole is so big that even electromagnetic waves like light can't get out of it...'** *(Part One)*. Stephens shows that Christopher, through the way he can simplify ideas, is able to deal with topics that most 15-year-olds do not study. The Maths Appendix reveals the clarity he can use to provide a solution to an A level Maths question. The mathematical language does not move the story forward, but it does bring closure and echoes the opening section when Christopher introduces himself by referring to his maths skills.

Christopher also shows how his literal understanding of other people's language creates difficulties for him. He understands what a metaphor is even though he does not understand specific metaphors. He cannot infer what people mean when they

LANGUAGE

use **figurative language** and therefore cannot respond to it. He is most comfortable when he can deal with evidence and truth. Neither does Christopher use language that describes emotions. He admits that he does not understand matters linked to feelings:

> **Key quotations**
>
> **Siobhan: It's because I'm not your mother... That's very important, Christopher. Do you understand that?**
>
> **Christopher: I don't know.** *(Part Two)*

figurative language the collective term for **simile**, metaphor, etc; language that is not to be taken literally

simile a comparison of one thing to another using the words 'like' or 'as'

The dialogue between Christopher and his father stops after the confession about Wellington. In Part Two, Christopher's only discussion with Ed takes place in his head when he is trying to work out how to get to London. That shows how Christopher imagines his father would respond to what he is doing and Stephens reflects the breakdown in the relationship through Ed's language: **'Don't... won't... How the hell... haven't... wrong place'** *(Part Two)*. These verbs carry connotations of negativity and refusal. The implied aggression in the use of the noun 'hell' and adjectival phrase 'wrong place' show Ed's feelings towards Christopher. Even by the end of Part Two, Ed only speaks to Christopher with Judy present. The responses he receives from Christopher are still largely negative: **'No. No. No. No. No. No you can't. No'** *(Part Two)*. The word 'no' is not part of a sentence. It could be regarded as an exclamation, as Christopher refuses Ed's request. Stephens repeats it to emphasize the strength of Christopher's feelings and to reinforce the hostility implied in the refusal.

Use of the first person

The entire play focuses on Christopher and so a high proportion of the story is told in the first person, giving his perspective of events. Stephens gives some of Christopher's words to Siobhan as she reads his book. The text of Christopher's book is a device that enables the audience to 'see' into his mind. It also allows the audience to gain an understanding of the impact he has on the people he interacts with as his words are delivered at secondhand, or third hand if they have been voiced by Siobhan.

LANGUAGE

Even as Siobhan is reading his own words from his book, Christopher concentrates on something he is passionate about

Christopher's speeches are dominated by use of the first person. Through this, Stephens is perhaps reflecting the obsessive nature of some autistic people and Christopher's inability to understand the feelings or needs of anyone else, e.g. **'I came home from school one day… so I went and found the secret key… I let myself into the house… I put the key in the bowl…'** *(Part One)*. This use of the first person conveys the way Christopher sees the world. For him, it is limited to his own interests and knowledge. He has little understanding of the wider world. This can be heard in the frequency of his references to himself: **'I didn't know… I like Wellington and I went to say hello to him…'** *(Part One)*. By the end of the play, Stephens shows that Christopher's perspective has expanded slightly through his use of plurals and the third person. This emphasizes Christopher's increasing maturity and broadening understanding.

Stephens shows Christopher's determination to make his life successful. He uses a range of **modal verbs** to express Christopher's desires and expectations about his future. Phrases such as 'I am going to…' and 'I will…' are repeated frequently to demonstrate his plans. Towards the end of the play, these verbs are moderated to 'I can…', which reflects the amended plans and also Christopher's improved understanding of what he is really capable of, rather than just what he wants.

> **modal verb** a verb such as 'can', 'may' or 'will' that is used with another verb to express possibility, permission, intention, etc.

Sentence structure

Stephens uses sentence structure to create a strong sense of personality in the speeches. The audience forms an opinion of the characters not just based on the words they use but also on the way they are spoken because of the sentence structure and punctuation.

LANGUAGE

Activity 4

Read Christopher's dialogue with Ed in Part One (including that spoken by Siobhan) from **'I think I would make a very good astronaut'** to **'a Dream Come True'**. How does the language Stephens uses in this section show Christopher's intelligence and also his difficulties? Choose three quotations, then copy and complete the table as a record of your ideas.

Quotation	Effect of language chosen	Linguistic features
'You have to be someone who would like being on their own... no one else in them with me' (Part One)	Stephens emphasizes that Christopher prefers to be alone by using two different expressions to explain it. This emphasizes how hard he finds relationships with other people and that isolation from them is not something he is worried about. He anticipates enjoying the time he would be in space as he would not have to deal with anyone else.	Repetition: language varies but repeats the same idea: 'on their own' and 'no one'. Both emphasize Christopher's preference to be alone.

At some points, Christopher uses very long sentences with minimal additional punctuation. This creates a flow of speech that indicates the fast-moving exploration of an idea, e.g. **'Then they worked out that the universe was expanding... which was why their light never reached us'** *(Part One)*. The context shows why Stephens gives Christopher this type of dialogue. This example occurs in the scene when Christopher has been arrested. He is describing to Ed what he could see as he was driven to the police station. He is in a stressful situation and the audience has already seen him react aggressively towards an authority figure. This sentence structure shows a level of intelligence in Christopher that has not yet been seen and also shows his ability to distract himself in challenging situations. The same technique is seen at other points in the play when Christopher is under stress.

At other points, Stephens uses short sentences to emphasize what is being said, e.g. **'It's going to be alright. Honestly. Trust me'** *(Part One)*. This brevity may be necessary to help Christopher understand what is being said to him when he is in a state of stress and unable to cope. Using more extended language would possibly create further complications he could not deal with. The example above contains an imperative, which shows that Ed is trying to exert some control over a situation that he recognizes has deteriorated badly.

Stephens also uses ellipsis to indicate the struggle Ed has when trying to explain why he did not tell Christopher the truth about his mother: **'... I thought she might carry on coming over... and maybe I was being stupid...'** *(Part One)*. The hesitancy this structure conveys reveals more about Ed's difficulties and helps the audience understand the source of his confusion. The repetition of ideas reveals that he is uncertain how to explain why he believed the situation was going to turn out differently.

> ### Activity 5
>
> Look at Ed's speech in Part One from **'Look maybe I shouldn't say this...'** to **'... turn out like this'**, when he tries to explain to Christopher what has happened and the decisions he made.
>
> What impact do the following features have on the audience? Write about:
>
> - the use of imagery
> - the use of sentence structure.

Writing about language

Upgrade

Stephens blends realistic dialogue conventions with precise scientific and mathematical language, which creates a unique understanding of the mind of an individual character.

In an exam, you need to show that you understand the impact of Stephens's choice of words. Some students do not write in enough detail about aspects of word choice and this is one reason why they do not gain high grades. This is particularly important if you are asked to write about an extract from the text. This gives you the opportunity to focus your attention on particular sections in detail. Try to refer to:

- reasons why Stephens may have chosen particular words or phrases
- the significance of the words in relation to the context and themes
- differences in the speech of different characters
- the impact on the audience of the different types of language used.

Themes

Honesty and truthfulness

From the opening scene Christopher makes clear his position on telling the truth: **'I do not tell lies. ...But it is not because I am a good person. It is because I can't tell lies'** *(Part One)*. He is consistent in this throughout the whole play. He also has similarly high expectations of other people, and it is this that leads to subsequent events.

Christopher pursues truth in order to discover who killed Wellington, and makes his family and neighbours uncomfortable in the process. No one else tells the truth in the same way as Christopher, who sticks just to the facts and seems unaffected by any emotional considerations. Unlike others, Christopher is also perfectly willing to contradict someone in order to stick to the truth:

> **Key quotations**
>
> **Siobhan: ... I never said that.**
>
> **Christopher: Yes you did.**
>
> **Siobhan: I didn't use those words Christopher.**
>
> **Christopher: You did on 12 September last year.** *(Part One)*

Christopher discusses with Siobhan his views on why people are hard to understand and cites use of metaphors and **idioms**, which are unclear to him. Christopher explains that he thinks that using these types of phrases is the same as lying because the person does not mean what they are saying. This foreshadows Ed's use of **euphemisms** to explain what happened to Judy, knowing that Christopher will not pick up on the subtleties of what he is saying: **'She has a problem... a problem with her heart'** *(Part One)*. Christopher accepts this at face value as Judy having had a heart attack. He does not realize that Ed is actually trying to say that Judy has fallen out of love with him and is in love with another person.

Both Ed and Judy are shown to have lied to Christopher. Judy is untruthful about her feelings, as shown in her affair with Roger; Ed lies about Judy and Wellington. Ed's lies attempt to cover up his killing of the dog and it is this that causes Christopher to lose trust in him. This trust has to be rebuilt and won again through the medium of utter honesty about what has happened: **'... I am going to tell you the truth from now on. About everything'** *(Part One)*. The audience understands why Ed told lies, as he was trying to protect his son from a complex problem that he was unsure how to explain. However, Stephens demonstrates that this 'web of lies', in the series of untruths told to Christopher, traps both Ed and Judy.

> **euphemism** a mild word or phrase used instead of an offensive or frank one
>
> **idiom** an expression where the overall meaning is different from that of the separate words that make it up

THEMES

Stephens explores the consequences of not being honest and shows the results on the Boone family of the lies that have been told. The impact of this upon the audience is to call into question the social lies that many people use to make life easier and seem less complicated. For example, people accept the telling of 'white lies' as an excuse to save someone's feelings from being hurt, perhaps in response to a question about appearance, hairstyle or an outfit. On a larger scale, many people feel it is acceptable to lie to an employer about illness in order to have an additional day off from work. This brings the audience back to the challenge posed by the author of the novel, Mark Haddon, that the play reveals more about ourselves than about Christopher.

> **Activity 1**
>
> Christopher cannot understand why his father lied. Look at Ed's speech in Part One from **'Look maybe I shouldn't say this…'** to **'… to turn out like this'**. Pick out three quotes that reveal things that Ed has concealed from Christopher. Write about each one, suggesting why you think Ed made the choice to lie about it.

Judy is shocked by Ed's lies, which suggests that he didn't lie when they lived together. However, she is also seen to be untruthful. She appears to have left home without telling Ed where she was going or what she was doing. Her letters show the audience the truth of her situation and feelings. As Christopher reads the letters, he and the audience learn simultaneously how hard she found the parting and how she felt about leaving: **'… it would be better for all of us if I went'** *(Part One)*. She chooses to leave home unexpectedly again after Roger tries to hit Christopher. Stephens shows that habits of concealment are hard to break and that both Ed and Judy have to work on their truthfulness.

Christopher, on the other hand, learns during the course of the play that complete honesty is not always necessary. At the beginning of the play, he is utterly honest but, as he matures and changes, he becomes able to conceal truth, e.g. **'I was just chatting'** *(Part One)*. This is not the same as lying but he has learned that a partial truth is enough in some cases, especially if used to cover up something he knows he should not have done.

Siobhan appears to be the most honest character. This may be due to the fact that she is employed to work with Christopher and, though clearly caring for him, she does not carry the same amount of emotional baggage as his parents. This seems to free her to speak truthfully to him, even if it is not what he wants to hear. Her truthfulness means that she keeps Christopher's trust despite all the changes he experiences, whereas his parents both have to work to re-establish his trust in them.

By the end of the play, when all the characters are aware of the truth of their situations, their lives return to a form of calm as they learn to coexist with each other by being honest. Members of the audience are left questioning their own honesty about what they tell their children and each other.

Activity 2

How does Stephens present ideas about honesty and truthfulness? Plan a response to this question. You may wish to create a spider diagram or plan each section of your response in bullet points. Try to include quotations and/or references to the text to support your ideas. Retain this plan for revision in preparation for your exam.

Difference

The play explores 'difference', as in the way society regards anyone who does not fit into conventional behaviour patterns. This includes, but is not limited to, Christopher.

Christopher is seen to be very different in his speech, behaviour, attitudes, social understanding and social skills. From early in the play, the audience can see that he does not represent a stereotypical teenager. However, other characters also cause the audience to question differences of opinions, in parenting styles and about lying.

Autism creates differences in people that prevent them from understanding the world in the same way as other people might do. The conflicts that arise from this can give autistic people significant problems. It is for this reason, not lack of intelligence, that Christopher attends a special school. However, the characters that are not autistic show that they view the world differently to each other. Ed is trapped by the lies he told his son whereas Judy is shown to be truthful about herself. Judy may be regarded as selfish in following her desire to live a different sort of life, while Ed remains in the family home making sure that Christopher's differences are accommodated.

Christopher sees the world in 'black and white' terms, unlike many other people. He has no 'grey' areas to confuse him. These grey areas present difficulties for the adult characters, who struggle to decide on appropriate responses or answers: **'And once I'd said that... I couldn't change it. It just... It got out of control'** *(Part One)*. At different points in the play Ed is seen to struggle to control his emotions. This contrasts with society's view of men as they are often expected to behave in ways that seem unemotional. Similarly, Judy has abandoned her child, which is contrary to society's expectations of mothers. Stephens uses these characteristics to show different approaches to a shared problem. Each character resolves their problems in an individual way, which others may find unacceptable.

The play also challenges the audience's perception of what 'difference' really means and makes us ask questions about our own 'difference' when compared to other people. In responding to the play, the writer of the novel Mark Haddon said '… I might say that *Curious* is not really about Christopher at all. It's about us.' Stephens shows what happens when different world views collide and suggests that resolving our differences can only be done with consent on all sides.

Key quotation

… when the red mist comes down… Christ, you know what I'm talking about. I mean we're not that different me and you… *(Ed, Part One)*

Activity 3

Ed and Judy have different parenting styles. Look back through the play and find information that shows you their differing approaches and attitudes to bringing Christopher up. Copy and complete the table below. You may be able to add other issues to the list. Keep your table to help with your exam revision.

Issue	Judy's response	Ed's response
Exam qualifications	Calls school to withdraw Christopher this year. Doesn't think it is important.	Argues with the headteacher about Christopher being able to do A level Maths.
Doing things outside the home		
Eating properly		
Being truthful		
Supporting ambitions		

Family relationships

At best, the Boone family might be described as somewhat dysfunctional, not being able to deal with normal social relationships or expectations.

- Ed is a single parent, who is shown to have real difficulties in controlling his temper on occasion and this sometimes descends into physical and emotional child abuse.
- Judy is an absent parent, allegedly dead, who is unable to cope with her own emotions and feelings to the extent that she leaves her son to follow her own desires.
- Christopher is a behaviourally challenged teenager struggling with being unable to understand other people and unable to express emotions at all. He lives in a self-centred world impinged on at different times by his parents' actions.

The complicated relationship between Ed and Judy is not shown in depth because the adults are seen through the perspective of the much younger and very unworldly Christopher. This puts the audience in the position of seeing them as he sees them. Revelations about the family are as much of a surprise to the audience as they are to Christopher. However, it is clear that Stephens places importance on the ways the individuals within families are interdependent. Even Christopher, who does not really understand the complexities of adult relationships, knows that family members should be able to rely on and trust each other.

THEMES

When trying to decide what to do about Ed having killed Wellington, he wants to stay with **'... a member of my family'** *(Part One)*. He dismisses those he knows only slightly and reverts to the unpredictable, but well-known Judy as the best option. A mother who has left him behind appears to be better than a father who cannot be trusted.

In his representation of family, Stephens seems to be reflecting aspects of modern Britain. In 2011, Contact A Family (a charity working with families of disabled children and young people) estimated that 25% of families with a disabled child end up experiencing a breakdown and up to 72% of parents in this situation suffer with anxiety or depression. Ed and Judy seem to typify a considerable number of parents trying to work out how best to deal with the changes and challenges of living with their disabled child. The accusations and blame that each seeks to place on the other may be a feature of their own struggles:

> **Key quotations**
>
> **Judy: What in God's name do you think you were playing at saying those things to him?**
>
> **Ed: You were the one that bloody left.** *(Part Two)*

Other characters involved with the Boone family offer a partial glimpse of other family relationship. However, these are never fully developed, perhaps reflecting the fact that it is not possible to understand what it is like to live in someone else's family. Mr Thompson's brother, who answers the door to Christopher, must look very similar to the actual neighbour and deals with Christopher quite firmly so he goes away; Mrs Alexander makes reference to her grandson, who is **'... almost your age'** *(Part One)*, but he is never seen nor mentioned again. Rhodri, Ed's work partner, appears briefly and knows the family well enough to tease Christopher, but there is no reference to his own domestic life. Christopher does mention his grandparents but, as **'three of them are dead and Grandma Burton... has senile dementia...'** *(Part One)*, there is no extended family to provide respite or support for the Boones. Stephens focuses on this single family and the relationships within this microcosm as a way of showing family tensions that might apply to many other families.

The conclusion of the play, when Ed and Christopher are both working to re-establish their relationship, seems to offer hope that their future happiness is bound up in being together as a family. Although Judy appears to be receding in importance to Christopher again (hence her lack of involvement with the gardening and the dog), she is known to be supporting Christopher to re-establish trust with Ed: **'Mother said I didn't have a choice'** *(Part Two)*. Ed has taken proactive steps to help Christopher understand that he is loved and that rebuilding trust is important to his father. He has also taken action to provide Christopher with educational goals, reinforcing his belief that his son can fulfil his career aspirations: Christopher says, **'He told Mrs Gascoyne that I'm going to take Further Maths next year'** *(Part Two)*.

Perhaps the most tangible **symbol** of the family rebuilding relationships is when Ed gives Christopher the puppy, clearly in consultation with Judy. The dog may represent a future that will continue to expand as Christopher becomes a young adult and shows that he will now be able to experience being a carer, not only being cared for, within the family. Even though he will only be caring for a dog, this shows a significant increase in maturity and also reinforces the value Christopher placed on his relationship with Wellington at the start of the play.

symbol a thing that represents or stands for something else

Activity 4

Siobhan is not a member of the Boone family, but has a strong relationship with Christopher. How far would you agree that her behaviour is similar to a parent's in the way she treats him? Try to write two paragraphs to explore this question. Use quotations and references to support your ideas.

Science and maths

Stephens makes it very clear that Christopher's areas of special interest are science and maths. His introduction of himself to the audience shows the extent of his knowledge, albeit in a very simple way: *'I know… every prime number up to 7507'* (Part One). Though an interesting fact about him, this does not reveal the true extent of his ability with maths. The audience learns this very gradually until the final scene when Christopher explains the A level problem he solved successfully in his exam.

Prime numbers

These numbers can only be divided by 1 and by themselves. For example, 7 can only be divided by 1 and by 7. The only even prime number is 2; the rest are odd.

Christopher uses maths, especially prime numbers, as a way of dealing with his anxiety. His knowledge of prime numbers is not just a clever party trick but serves a practical purpose for him. He recites numbers, for example, in order to help him calm his breathing, cope with the exams and deal with catching a train. He likes the certainty of the sequences. He knows numbers will not change

Christopher uses prime numbers to calm his anxiety on the journey to find his mother

THEMES

depending on their mood, will never lie to him and cannot surprise him by doing the unexpected. As Marcus du Sautoy (Professor of Mathematics at Oxford University) wrote, 'Mathematics has a security and permanence about it that is comforting in a world of uncertainty and ambiguity'. Christopher is sure that he can cope with the demands of A level exams because he is so confident about his ability: **'I'm going to do A level Maths next month. And I'm going to get an A*'** *(Part Two)*. Stephens shows this in sharp contrast to Christopher's social communication skills when he has to deal with other people who are not predictable or stable.

Christopher's interest in science is revealed when he starts to discuss the nature of the universe with Ed. He has been arrested and when Ed arrives at the police station to collect him, he wants to talk about what he has seen from the police car and what he knows about stars: **'… they worked out that the universe was expanding, that the stars were all rushing away from one another after the Big Bang…'** *(Part One)*. Ed is unimpressed, perhaps because he understands that this is a form of diversion to stop Christopher having to think about where he is or what has happened to him. It provides a break from reality and allows Christopher to feel comfortable in a world of his own choosing.

The Dream that Christopher has about working in science or possibly being an astronaut is more fully revealed when he speaks about this after a row with Ed about his ongoing investigations.

Activity 5

Read the episode in Part One from **'I think I would make a very good astronaut…'** to **'… a Dream Come True'** when Christopher/Siobhan talks about being an astronaut. Using the information in that section, explain how Christopher thinks his needs will be met by being an astronaut. You could use the example below as your starting point.

Annotations	Response
Makes a better word choice, showing understanding that space holds more than just an interest for Christopher.	Christopher has clearly researched the work done by an astronaut as he is able to refer to a number of features he finds ~~interesting~~ attractive because of his individual needs. He first describes needing to be 'intelligent' and 'understanding… machines', both of which he knows he can demonstrate. These comments are developed more fully as he continues to explain the nature of the attraction of space. Christopher is unusual as he likes small spaces, something many people do not like. His next comment reveals more about his needs…
Shortened quotations are more appropriate to this response.	
Shows awareness of Christopher's difference.	
Focuses on the question again.	

Using the logic of maths and science enables Christopher to address solving the cause of Wellington's death in a similar way to solving mathematical or scientific problems. He applies his knowledge of events and finds evidence to support his ideas.

He works through all the possible outcomes and so moves in the direction of solving the problem. He uses facts to support what he does rather than being affected by emotion. This also allows him to move beyond his known, safe environment into the wider world as he applies the same principles of observation and logic to find his mother's flat: *'… watch the people. It's easy look. You go to the black machine…'* *(Part Two)*. This proves to him that he could do more in the future. Science and maths are the two things in Christopher's life that remain constants, even when all else lets him down, and he concludes the play by demonstrating to the audience how he can make his favourite subject interesting to everyone.

Maths Appendix

Though only a very small part of the play (slightly over 6 minutes), this finale shows Christopher's speed of thought and ability to make a complex problem clear. Stephens uses stage directions to support Christopher's presentation and ensure that it is transparent even to those who are not mathematically inclined: *'Using as much theatricality as we can throw at it, using music, lights, sound, lasers…'*. Christopher speaks directly to the audience, still in role, breaks down the question into simpler steps and demonstrates how his answer is correct.

Stephens uses the maths problem to show how Christopher might be able to take on the challenges of studying at university and working as a scientist. He is transformed by his knowledge and the opportunity to explain his obsession to willing listeners. The audience is forced to recognize the difference between their own ability in this subject and Christopher's, so the play concludes with his maths ability in the ascendant. In addition, Stephens shows the audience what it is like to not understand something that another person takes for granted, in the same way that Christopher experienced life previously.

Activity 6

Simon Baron-Cohen (Director of the Autism Research Centre, Cambridge University) states in his article 'Christopher and Asperger's Syndrome' that 'He [Christopher]… derives a sense of peace and satisfaction from the beauty of mathematics'.

Identify two key points in the play when Christopher shows he uses maths to create peace and/or satisfaction. Explain how Stephens presents these moments and what the impact is on the audience.

Activity 7

Choose at least one of the linked themes below and create your own revision notes on your chosen theme(s). Think carefully about how Stephens presents the theme.

- Honesty and truthfulness
- Family relationships
- Difference
- Science and maths

Performance

The play was first performed in London in 2012 and this National Theatre production ran at various London theatres until June 2017, when it then toured the UK. This production won seven Olivier Awards, including for best new play. The play was also performed in various other countries, including a two-year run on Broadway in New York.

The performance of a play is the ultimate goal of any playwright. Plays are written to present ideas and challenge audiences to think about wider aspects of life. In adapting the novel of *The Curious Incident of the Dog in the Night-Time*, Simon Stephens wanted to bring the same honesty and clarity to the stage version that he felt had been in the book. Marianne Elliott, director of the play, felt that adapting the novel was 'risky' because people who had read the book might find that their views of the story were not the same as what was portrayed on stage.

One of the aspects Stephens felt it was important to retain was the quality of the dialogue that Mark Haddon had written, because the characters use conversation to make an impression on other characters. However, using just dialogue would not have been sufficient to create Christopher's world without considering how the performance would also help audiences understand more about the characters.

Tips for assessment

Upgrade

Watching a performance of the play, whether live, streamed, online or filmed, will help you to understand how the characters' dialogue and actions work together. It allows you to hear the tone each character uses so you can gain a better understanding of their mood. You can also see the way a character behaves and therefore understand their personality better. This may help you when you are responding to questions about individual characters. Search online for more information about the National Theatre production or touring versions of the play.

Creating the roles

The director would have worked closely with Stephens and the actors to ensure that the whole production and the characters on stage fulfilled the playwright's purpose in writing the play.

Physicality

Actors are trained to use their bodies to communicate. Body language can tell an audience a lot about a character without using words. The audience makes a judgement about each character based on the way the actor moves in relation to the space and other actors. Creating a character physically involves using:

- gestures – movement of the hands to convey information
- movement – gait, posture and interaction with other characters
- facial expression – movement of the face to show mood and reactions to events.

PERFORMANCE

Most members of an audience do these things when they interact with other people, but unconsciously. However, most of us are experts at understanding what gestures, movement and facial expression convey about a person. Actors have the skill to adopt these to make characters appear to be using them naturally. This process is often referred to as **physicality**.

In the National Theatre productions, the actor playing Christopher had to use a different set of gestures, movements and facial expressions to the other characters.

> **closed gesture** small controlled movement
> **physicality** use of the body to show mood/feelings

He tried to present a teenager who has Asperger syndrome. As part of his research for the role, Luke Treadaway, the original actor, observed young people in a special school to study their movements and behaviour. He then used his observations to portray a young man who has small, **closed gestures**, uses few facial expressions and moves in very controlled ways. These factors created an image of Christopher's difference as well as showing the audience that he finds it difficult to express himself.

Another aspect of the physicality required can be seen when Christopher is touched or when his parents show him affection without touching. Christopher's extreme reactions to touch by others need to be planned and rehearsed so that they look natural and spontaneous. The fact that he can barely tolerate his parents touching him, for example, is shocking because of their family relationship. So the touching of fingertips reinforces how hard each character finds the situation but also allows the audience to see that affection can be expressed in alternative ways. This gesture is used to startling effect when Ed reveals that he killed Wellington:

Luke Treadaway made small movements, like twisting a hoodie cord, seem natural for Christopher

'Ed *holds his right hand up for* Christopher *to touch*. Christopher *ignores it.* Ed *stares at* Christopher' *(Part One)*. It is the lack of touch here that reveals each character's feelings and shows the audience what this withdrawal means to each of them.

PERFORMANCE

Gestures and physicality also convey the level of stress that Christopher feels at different points. His unusual behaviour in response to events is another characteristic that demonstrates how he differs from other teenagers. This behaviour includes repeated rocking, hitting the floor or himself, fiddling with his fingers and putting his hands over his ears to block out sound. All these are atypical behaviours but help the audience understand how difficult the character finds a situation.

Activity 1

Choose one character (not Christopher) and write about how physicality could be used to express their personality, thoughts and feelings. First, consider how you use each of the following to express your own personality:

- gestures
- movement
- facial expression.

Then explain how each might be used to help portray the character you have chosen.

Key quotation

He crouches down. He rolls himself into a ball. He starts hitting his hand and his feet and his head against the floor... (Part One)

Unconventional movement

When Stephens transformed the novel into the play, he wanted to reveal Christopher's inner world to the audience. He was keen that this should be done as effectively as possible on stage.

One of the ways this was achieved in the National Theatre production was to collaborate with the company Frantic Assembly. This company focuses on the physical aspects of performance and uses the actors' bodies in new and experimental ways. Its aim is to collaborate with performers to make theatre more dynamic and exciting. The results are more like **choreography**. The actors are trained to use movements to show the audience a range of emotions and events from new perspectives. This type of performance places demands on the actors that they may not experience in other productions.

choreography sequences of moves and steps for a dance

PERFORMANCE

The National Theatre production of *The Curious Incident of the Dog in the Night-Time* required the whole company to move in surprising ways to show the workings of Christopher's mind and emotions more clearly. Each actor, except the one playing Christopher, had to take other roles in addition to their specific character.

Early in the play, as Christopher explains to Siobhan about his mother, the members of the cast portray inanimate objects such as a door or a chair. This shows the audience how Christopher's world is limited to the things that are important to him. The objects disappear once he has finished with them and the cast members resume their character roles. Christopher does not notice when the characters or the objects are not there.

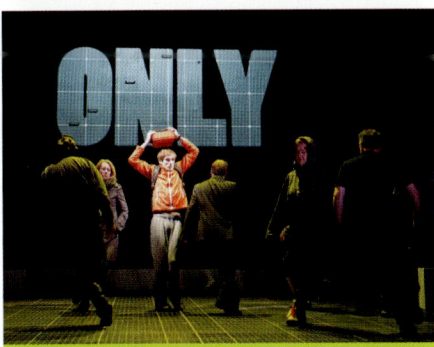

Christopher and Toby travel through space

The way Christopher acts marks him out as different

In order to show Christopher's fantasy of travelling through space with Toby, other actors support them so that the teenager and his rat actually seem to be drifting, weightless, through space.

At other times, the whole company moves together to reflect Christopher's state of mind. For example, when Christopher is lost on the tube in London, all the actors except him move like a crowd, walking in one direction while he tries to push through the opposite way. He does not move in the same way as the rest of the cast, so this emphasizes his vulnerability and confusion.

Activity 2

Re-read Siobhan's speech in Part One from **'Mother died…'** to **'… best ever score'**. Think about how you could perform this sequence of events without using any props but only bodies to show what Christopher is doing.

- What difficulties would you face in showing Christopher's actions?
- What directions might you give the actor playing Christopher so the events were consistent with the speech?

PERFORMANCE

Voice

Reading a script allows anyone to understand what the characters say on a very straightforward level. However, the way an actor uses their voice is a very important factor in creating a character. They use tone, **pace**, volume and accent to help the audience understand their character's intentions and emotions. This can make the performance memorable. In addition, actors must deliver lines clearly enough for everyone to hear and understand, avoiding the shortened forms we accept in everyday speech so that the audience does not miss important parts of the dialogue. Character is created as much by how the words are spoken as by the actual words used.

Christopher speaks in a **monotone**, sometimes without apparently pausing for breath, e.g. **'Wellington is a dog that used to belong to my neighbour Mrs Shears who is our friend but he is dead now because somebody killed him by putting a garden fork through him…'** *(Part One)*. This is partly because of the sentence structure Stephens uses but it is also due to the way the director and actor interpret the character. The actor has to deliver these lines quickly enough to give an impression of Christopher's feelings but not so quickly that the meaning and important information is lost.

Actors also make other sounds with the voice, which are not actual words, to make their characters seem realistic. In everyday speech, people use non-verbal cues to show others their feelings, including noises that indicate agreement, support or interest. However, Christopher groans and moans to express the stress he is experiencing: **'Christopher *is moaning still in his ball*…'** *(Part Two)*. He is not able to articulate his feelings so he expresses them by making sounds. This shows the audience how difficult social communication is for Christopher. Moaning and groaning are often interpreted as signs of pain or unhappiness so their use reinforces our understanding of Christopher and the situations he is trying to deal with.

> **monotone** a single, unvarying tone of voice
> **pace** the speed at which someone speaks

Activity 3

a) Re-read Siobhan's speech in Part One from **'When I started writing my book…'** to **'… WRONG CONCLUSIONS'**. Consider what moods could be shown at this point in the play, e.g. angry, excited, sad or happy. Read the speech aloud again in different tones, varying the pace and volume to create different impressions.

b) What do the different tones, paces and volumes suggest about the character and the situation? Which do you think are most suited to conveying the impression you want? Record your observations about the effects of each variation so you can use your notes for revision purposes.

Timing

Delivering lines at the right time, alongside appropriate movements and action, is crucial to help the audience understand the impact of the words. Stephens includes directions about the timing of delivery as part of the script: *'The Duty Sergeant looks at him for a beat'* (Part One). The effect of a pause like this shows the audience what the character is experiencing. Here, the Duty Sergeant has to think about the most suitable response to the troubled teenager before him.

In other places, lines are delivered more quickly to show that tension is being built up. Stephens uses Judy's letters to explain her reasons for leaving and the delivery of these speeches, alongside Christopher's actions, show how she felt less and less able to cope. Christopher is shown building his train set as she speaks, so there is no interaction between them, but the direction *'His building becomes frantic. At times almost balletic'* (Part One) suggests his internal struggle. Stephens's request for 'frantic' and 'balletic' action brings out the mixed emotions Christopher appears to be feeling. However, if the speech and actions were not delivered as a timed sequence, the effect would not be the same.

Timing can also combine with tone of voice to deliver humour. In normal conversation, it is possible to suggest something is amusing through the way it is said. The words themselves may not be funny, but the timing and delivery of the lines create amusement. Sometimes the humour is created because of the mismatch between a character's expectations and what actually happens or is said. At other times, humour is created visually through a facial expression or movement.

> **Activity 4**
>
> The actor Luke Treadaway, who played Christopher originally, suggested that humour is essential when responding to the play otherwise the whole piece becomes too bleak and depressing.
>
> To what extent do you agree with his evaluation of the play as bleak and depressing? Write a few paragraphs arguing either for or against this viewpoint.

Staging

The National Theatre production used the standard features of staging – set, lighting, sound effects – in different and quite ground-breaking ways. Marianne Elliott, the director, and Bunny Christie, the set designer, wanted the staging to reflect Christopher's mind so they dispensed with many of the features that audiences might expect to see, including furniture, doors for entrances and exits, and painted scenery. Instead, the set resembled the inside of a box, which contained everything needed for the play, in the same way that Christopher's mind provided everything he needed to succeed. The set is a metaphor for Christopher.

PERFORMANCE

The inside of the 'box' appeared to be made of dark graph paper, with boxes around the illuminated edges of the set. The walls and floor of the stage became part of the way the story unfolds. Christopher drew designs on the floor in a way that is reminiscent of mathematicians drawing diagrams, scientists working out calculations on a blackboard or even police officers compiling a 'suspect' board. Parts of the walls and floor opened, like cupboards, to reveal objects that were taken out for use and then returned later. The effect was to make the performing space seem both self-contained and yet open to possibilities, reflecting Christopher's mind as he grapples with both these aspects of his personality.

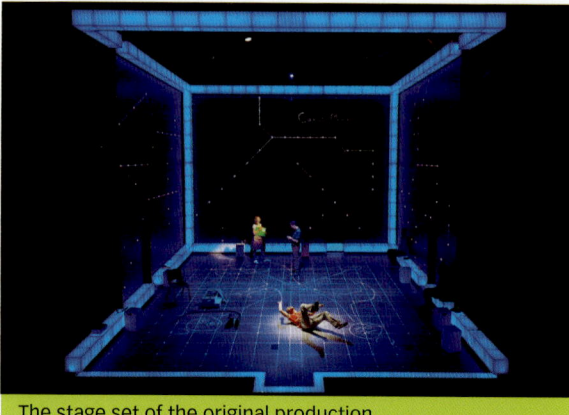

The stage set of the original production

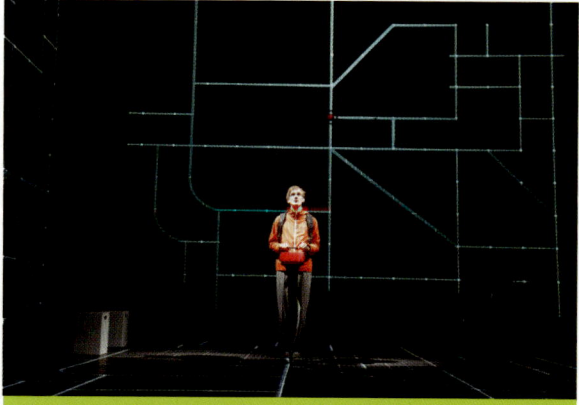

Lighting was used to trace Christopher's journey and projected images and words, combined with multi-layered sound effects of voices and music, revealed the muddle that Christopher perceives to be around him. This produced sensory overload, so any audience would struggle to keep up with the change of pace and noise levels. Stephens and Elliott intended this unsettling effect to echo the difficulties that Christopher faced when dealing with what most people assume is normal life.

Lighting on the back wall traces Christopher's journey

Not many actual props were used, but the use of a series of pale-coloured blocks instead of traditional furniture was more effective. Because the blocks were uniform in shape and design, they could represent chairs, luggage and a luggage rack without distracting the eye or detracting from the unfolding events.

Elliott felt that staging the play in this way allowed the audience to focus much more on the story that was unfolding rather than being distracted by scenery or worrying about the timeline being followed. She was proved to have made the right decision when the play won the Olivier Award for best design, sound and lighting in 2013.

Activity 5

Re-read the stage directions at the end of Part Two from *'Using as much theatricality as we can throw at it...'* to the end. What do Stephens's directions show about how he wants the Maths Appendix to be delivered to the audience? Write a paragraph about the impact of the stage directions, focusing on key words and ideas. Write in as much detail as you would about a character's speech.

Activity 6

a) Create revision notes about the performance of the play using the information in this section.

b) If you have seen the play, add notes on the presentation of the drama and how it affected your understanding of the events. If you have not seen the play, you may find it useful to watch some short extracts online and then make notes about your impression of the staging and how it affects your perceptions of the characters.

Writing about performance

When studying a play, it is useful to consider the playwright's reasons for presenting the story as a play. The novel *The Curious Incident of the Dog in the Night-Time* was already well established and admired before the story was turned into a play. However, Stephens has spoken about his desire to create an experience for the audience that was different to reading the book.

When writing about the playwright's intentions for an exam question, you need to remember that the question will focus on the play not the novel. Your answers should therefore only refer to the play text. Describing the creation of the characters and the way they are presented may be a way to address some questions because this will demonstrate your ability to understand that you are the audience for the drama as well as the reader of the play text.

Skills and Practice

Exam skills

Perhaps the most important, most obvious and most overlooked thing you can do to succeed in your exam is to read the play several times!

Though necessary and useful, reading the play in class, with your teacher, should only be the first stage in developing an understanding and confidence you can show when it comes to the exam. There is no substitute for reading the play by yourself, taking some time to think about the issues it raises and considering what you learn or take away from that reading.

Supplement reading the play with reading around it. This may take the form of using a study guide such as this one or a revision guide, which will prompt you with further questions and techniques. You may also find it useful to do some research into the issues the play deals with or to access online articles to support your understanding of the context and Stephens's ideas. Reliable websites, developed by knowledgeable academic tutors, can also be useful in helping you to understand the wider context of the play.

The second most important thing for success is to make sure that you read the question carefully before starting to do any writing. There are a number of words and phrases that you will see recurring on practice questions. These imitate the questions you will get in your exam and will help you prepare for writing an answer that is clear and meets the examiner's expectations.

Understanding the question

As you read through the question, there are two things you need to consider:

- What is the question about?
- What am I expected to do?

Examiners complain that some students may have written an interesting essay but have not answered the question. The marks awarded will depend on you writing about the correct topic and extract. Underline or highlight the key words in the question to make sure you keep your focus firmly on those areas.

There are some key words and phrases that you need to understand as you tackle the questions:

'**How does the writer/Stephens…**' You are being asked to explain the ways that Stephens puts forward his ideas. You may need to refer to specific techniques and discuss the effects those create or you may need to pick out aspects of the language chosen and explore the impact that certain words have on the audience. You may be able to show how a character is revealed through the dialogue and the events that occur.

'**Explore…**' You are being asked to look at a topic from a number of different viewpoints and ask questions about it. You may be able to show different characters' attitudes to or perceptions of the topic. You may be able to suggest the viewpoint Stephens wanted the audience to agree with or accept.

SKILLS AND PRACTICE

'**Present…**' This word is often linked with the playwright, e.g. 'How does Stephens present parenting?' You are being asked to look at a theme, or a character, as shown throughout the play. It may be a changing feature, so you should consider how the topic develops from the beginning to the end of the play. For example, you might be able to show your understanding by discussing the differences in parenting styles between Judy and Ed at the start and at the end of the play. You would be expected to provide examples from the whole book with a focus on the particular topic, picking out examples of how Stephens uses language and events to show how each character parents Christopher.

'**How far do you agree?**' You will need to consider the topic or quotation provided, and then decide your own opinion about it. You will need to show that you can consider both sides of an argument, evaluate the different views and then come to a conclusion about why you do or do not agree with the question. For example:

> 'The play presents a depressing portrait of family life.' How far do you agree with this statement?

You should write about the behaviour and attitudes of the family members but also show how each character's actions impact on the others. You should also consider the themes of honesty and truthfulness to provide a full response. In your conclusion, you would need to return to the original statement about family life and give your considered and explained opinion.

'**In this extract… elsewhere**' You might find that you are given an extract from the play to write about before moving on to a more general theme or topic. It is probable that the first part of the question will direct you to write about the extract, before moving on to consider the text as a whole. To ensure that you have written about the key aspects of the extract, carefully read it through and consider how the question applies to that particular section of the play. You then need to select other sections or events to write about. You could choose a section that contrasts with the extract, perhaps providing an alternative view, as well as another section that extends the original point. Check if the question tells you how many other sections you need to write about; e.g. 'Explore at least two moments…' implies that two is the minimum you should write about. In this case, aim to use three, but no more than five, other passages in your answer.

'**In what ways…**' You are expected to use a range of examples to demonstrate how a theme or idea is shown. The references you provide should be taken from the whole play rather than focusing on only one or two examples. You are also expected to consider a range of ways something may occur. For example:

> In what ways are animals presented as equal to humans?

SKILLS AND PRACTICE

To answer this question, you would be expected to provide several examples of how Christopher treats animals from the beginning to the end of the play, and how Stephens uses language to explain the different attitudes of other characters.

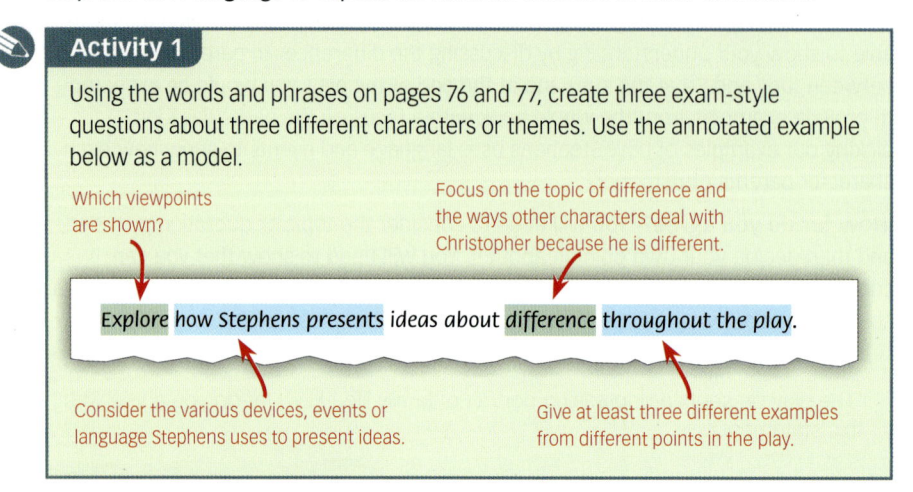

> **Activity 1**
>
> Using the words and phrases on pages 76 and 77, create three exam-style questions about three different characters or themes. Use the annotated example below as a model.
>
> Which viewpoints are shown?
>
> Focus on the topic of difference and the ways other characters deal with Christopher because he is different.
>
> Explore how Stephens presents ideas about difference throughout the play.
>
> Consider the various devices, events or language Stephens uses to present ideas.
>
> Give at least three different examples from different points in the play.

Planning your answer

There is a well-known saying that is often quoted to students around exam time, sometimes called the Six Ps – 'Planning and preparation prevents pathetically poor performance!'

Taking the time to plan your answer can make the difference between a well-organized and thoughtful response, and one that has good ideas but is disjointed and 'waffly'. By planning what you are going to include and thinking in advance which sections to refer to, you will be able to focus on choosing the best vocabulary and organizing your points logically.

You are more likely to impress the examiner by using your own views about the play rather than relying on what you have learned from your teacher or other students. Answers that show the ability to reflect on the themes and purpose of the writer score higher marks. Plan to write well in the exam by practising these skills in advance – your preparation time will enable you to feel confident about your ability when you are under pressure.

Plans can come in a variety of forms. These need doing before you attempt to write your full answer. Planning in retrospect, to try and show the examiner you have done it, is worthless as it simply takes up time better used to read through your work. That strategy could also throw up things you forgot to include and make you panic!

Bullet points and lists

Writing a list or bullet points can allow you to get your initial thoughts down very quickly and is probably the simplest form of planning.

Once you have created a list of ideas, you need to go back to the question and check that each item will answer what you are being asked. You may then need to reorganize the sequence to present the ideas in a more logical manner. Check over your list and decide if you need to move ideas into a more sequential order. Cross out any ideas you no longer think are relevant.

Next, try to add a short phrase or note to each point in your list to prompt your thoughts when it comes to writing the full answer. At this point, decide which sections of the text you will use to support each point.

Re-read the question before starting to write, using the list to remind you of your direction.

Activity 2

How does Stephens present Siobhan as a compassionate character?

Consider what you are being asked to write in response to this question. Allow yourself two minutes to jot down a list of ideas or points you think would be relevant. Take a further three minutes to complete the sequencing and identify appropriate sections of the play to use.

Spider diagrams

If you are a person who prefers to plan in a more visual manner, a spider diagram may help you to sort out your ideas. This allows you to get down a number of linked ideas quite quickly. Having done that, you would then need to decide on an appropriate order to write about each one.

You need to be sure you include the necessary aspects of the question so that the plan reminds you to write about Stephens's techniques as well as the 'compassionate' element.

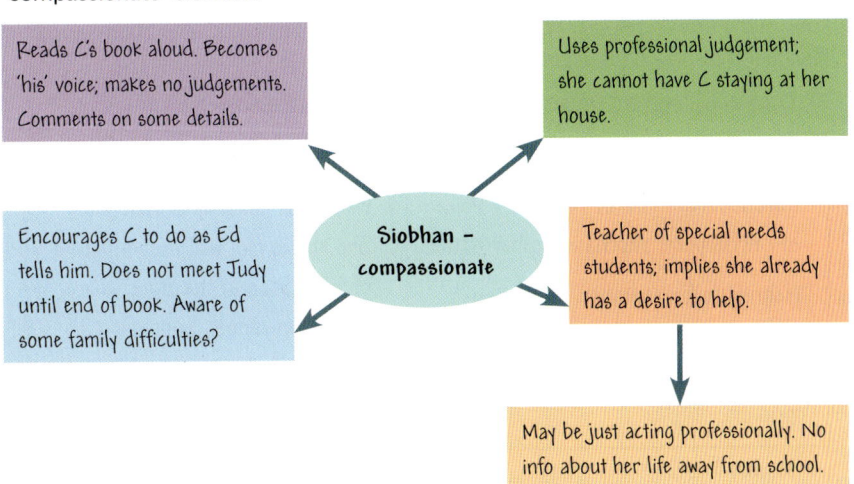

Reads C's book aloud. Becomes 'his' voice; makes no judgements. Comments on some details.

Uses professional judgement; she cannot have C staying at her house.

Encourages C to do as Ed tells him. Does not meet Judy until end of book. Aware of some family difficulties?

Siobhan – compassionate

Teacher of special needs students; implies she already has a desire to help.

May be just acting professionally. No info about her life away from school.

SKILLS AND PRACTICE

Activity 3

Experiment with planning by creating a spider diagram for each of the questions below. Try to include some quotations or references to particular sections that would be appropriate to support your points.

> 'The main lesson learned from the play is that no one can be completely honest.' How far do you agree with the statement?

> Explore how Stephens presents ideas about dealing with change throughout the play.

Six-box method

It is sometimes useful to create a more structured plan as it can provide more security and include more detail. The six-box method involves dividing ideas for your answer into six sections, including your introduction and conclusion, and mapping them out in a grid. This allows you to write notes rather than single words and phrases in your planning. Dividing the task into smaller sections also allows you to allocate time to the task and move through it smoothly. The more detailed information in each box can be reassuring if you suddenly find your mind has gone blank or you lose focus.

Activity 4

Look at the example below, based on the question in Activity 2. Some of the boxes have been completed as examples.

a) Copy and complete boxes 3, 4 and 5 to show what else could be included.

b) Discuss this as a method of planning. Do you prefer this to lists and bullet points?

1. Introduction – role of Siobhan = voice of Christopher; alternate mother figure. Techniques/presentation – Stephens's use of action/language at the start. Compassion shown through ways of speaking.	2. Behaviour towards Christopher. She knows him well over a period of time. Seen at the start as a teacher in school. Supports C's aspirations about maths/science. Gives him exam results.
3. Mother figure	4. Reader of C's diary

SKILLS AND PRACTICE

5. No character development. No life outside school shown.	6. Conclusion – recap on question. Her compassion shown more as situation becomes more serious. Stephens shows her professional distance but also emotional involvement; she provides stability for Christopher.

It is important to choose the method of planning that works for you. Which of these three methods of planning do you prefer and why?

Tips for assessment

Upgrade

Planning should take only a short amount of time. Avoid spending more than five to seven minutes planning or it could have a negative impact on your writing time.

Look back at your plan after writing each section of your answer to make sure you are still on track. Tick off each point as you write about it so you avoid repeating points.

Do not cross out your plan. If you run out of time, something you have included in the plan but did not have time to write about may help the examiner to understand how you were going to conclude.

Writing your answer

After planning your answer, you should move on to write the essay. You will have practised this in the months before the exam, so should be familiar with the expected structure:

- an introduction to address the question
- several linked paragraphs dealing with your points/arguments
- a conclusion to bring ideas together and ensure the question is answered.

You will need to use quotations from the text and references to the play at all stages of the writing.

You will need to show you understand that Stephens:

- wrote the play for a specific purpose
- chose the language to create particular effects
- was influenced by the context when he wrote
- intended the audience to have their ideas challenged.

Part of the mark for this question is given for spelling, punctuation and grammar. You need to check that what you have written is as clear as you can make it. To do this, you may find it useful to read each paragraph after finishing it and correct any mistakes straightaway.

SKILLS AND PRACTICE

Using an extract

Some exam questions provide a short extract from the play text, with the first part of the question specifically directing you to use that extract first. You will then be expected to link it with the rest of the play. The extract will have been selected to provide you with enough to write about in answer to the question.

1. Read the question first and think about what you are being asked to write about.
2. Read the extract carefully.
3. Re-read the question.
4. Return to the extract and identify which parts you can use to answer the question:
   - What is happening at this part of the play that is new?
   - How has Stephens used language and devices for effect?
   - How is the structure linked to the whole play?
   - Are there references to the context?
   - Which themes come out that link to the question?
5. Highlight or underline parts you consider will be relevant to answering the question. Make notes in the margins to remind you how you will use that section.
6. Plan your answer quickly using the notes and highlighted/underlined parts.
7. Write your answer.

Look at the exam-style question and extract on page 83. The extract has been annotated to show how you could approach this type of question.

SKILLS AND PRACTICE

Explore how Stephens presents Judy as a mother in the extract and elsewhere in the play.

Judy: 451c Chapter Road London NW2 5NG 02088878907. I was looking through some old photos last night, which made me sad. Then I found a photo of you playing with the train set we bought for you a couple of Christmases ago. And that made me happy because it was one of the really good times we had together. Do you remember how you played with it all day and you refused to go to bed at night because you were still playing with it. We told you about train timetables and you made a train timetable. And there was a little wooden station, too, and we showed you how people who wanted to go on the train went to the station and bought a ticket and then got on a train? And you played with it for weeks and weeks and weeks. I liked remembering that a lot.

Annotations:

- Judy's address. C memorizes it from her letters for when he needs it.
- Repeats verb. Refers to much younger C; infers he was less complicated to deal with.
- Judy's emotional state. Simple emotions described; knows C won't understand anything more complex?
- One... good times. Suggests there weren't many in her memory; links to her reasons for leaving Ed.
- Reflects on how hard she found C to manage; him didn't comply with her expectations.
- Foreshadows C going to London by train. Shows he knows what to do as he learned it from playing.
- Rhetorical question. Trying to engage C with shared memory so he understands the emotion.
- Repetition emphasizes C obsessing over things to the exclusion of all else. Links to difficulties with stopping doing an activity, e.g. investigating Wellington's death.

Activity 5

a) Re-read the question above. Then use the annotated extract to write the first section of an answer to the question. Focus on using appropriate examples from this extract.

b) Which other sections of the play would you link your ideas with? The annotations are only one person's suggestions. Try to identify other parts that would be equally useful.

Using quotations and references

Being able to select and use quotations and references that precisely support your point is an important skill in writing answers in the exam. Examiners will expect to see that you have used both direct quotations and references to parts of the text. This means you will need to paraphrase, writing what the characters say in your own words, as well as quote.

SKILLS AND PRACTICE

When you make a comment about a character, theme or idea, you need to show that you know that because of something Stephens wrote in the play. In the second part of your answer to the question on page 83, you need to show your knowledge of Judy as a mother in other parts of the play, so you could use a link like this:

> Stephens shows some facets of Judy through her letters. In a different letter, she writes about problems caused for them both because she found Christopher hard to deal with.

There are several examples you could choose to support this point, but to show that you are familiar with the whole play, select a quotation from a different point. One example could be:

> Judy recalls an argument at home when Christopher responds to her aggressively, saying, '... you grabbed the chopping board and you threw it ... and broke my toes' (Part Two). Christopher caused actual physical harm, and at that point Judy started to realize that her parenting skills were not the same as Ed's...

If you can, try to embed your quotations into your sentences, as in the example above. This makes the comment seem more fluent.

Remembering precise quotations may be a challenge in an exam situation. On occasion, it is acceptable to paraphrase in order to make your point. This is preferable to offering no support for a point. For example:

> Judy has not seen Christopher for two years and when she does find him outside her flat she appears to have forgotten one of his main problems – hatred of being touched – as she goes to hug him and is told not to.

Stephens' stage direction is actually, **'He pushes her away...'** (Part Two), but the sense of what the student has written is very similar and shows an understanding that Christopher rebuffs her.

SKILLS AND PRACTICE

Activity 6

Without using the play text, write the next section of the answer to the same question. Select another section that shows Judy as a mother so that you can add information to what has already been written.

Tips for assessment

Upgrade

Success in your exam will require you to do a number of things:

- Write confidently about the text using your own opinions and your own response. Examiners are interested in what you think about the play and your ability to explain those views.
- Offer some critical analysis of the text. This may be a developed argument on the question topic or a reflection about the writer's success in showing their viewpoint.
- Explore the 'message' of the text. Show you can explore some of the writer's concerns by focusing on the question and using precise references to support your ideas.
- Explore the way the writer has written the text. Analyse the language and style chosen by the writer.
- Choose precise quotations to support your points. These need to be embedded in your writing for maximum impact. Avoid using long quotations. These cannot show analysis in the same detail as a shorter one.
- Show an excellent understanding of the context of the text by referring to relevant issues around the time it was written and how these could have affected the writer and the audience.
- Use subject-specific vocabulary to explore your ideas. This shows you can explain your points with accuracy and clarity.
- Write in well-structured sentences and paragraphs, which use punctuation correctly.
- Spell even less common words accurately. Practise and learn subject-specific words before the exam.

SKILLS AND PRACTICE

Sample questions

1

Use the extract below and your knowledge of the whole play to answer the question.

Look at the extract from Part One from 'Could you take your laces out...' to '... your father's phone number Christopher?'

Write about the ways Christopher responds to police authority and how his responses are presented at different points in the play.

In your response you should:

- refer to the extract and the play as a whole
- show your understanding of characters and events in the play.

2

How does Stephens present Christopher as an atypical teenager in the play?

Write about:

- the ways Christopher behaves as an atypical teenager
- how Stephens presents Christopher in the play.

3

'This is good Christopher. It's quite exciting. I like the details.'

Explain how Stephens presents Siobhan as a positive influence in Christopher's life. You must refer to the whole text in your answer.

4

Use the extract below and your knowledge of the whole play to answer the question.

Look at the extract from Part One from 'I am going to find out who killed Wellington....' to ' ... You could very well say that'.

Explore how Stephens shows the significance of animals to Christopher in the extract and elsewhere in the play.

5

How does Stephens show the importance of family relationships? Refer to the whole play in your answer.

SKILLS AND PRACTICE

6 Use the extract below and your knowledge of the whole play to answer the question.

Look at the extract from Part One from 'I was really confused…' to '… Mother had died'.

Show how the difficult relationship between Christopher and his mother is presented in the play.
Write about:
- how Stephens presents Christopher and his mother in this extract
- how he presents the difficult relationship between Christopher and his mother in the play as a whole.

7 How does Stephens present Christopher dealing with change?
Write about:
- how Christopher deals with changes
- how Stephens presents Christopher's attitudes and feelings towards change.

8 'The play shows that students with Asperger syndrome should be educated in mainstream schools to give them the best chance of success.'
To what extent do you agree with this statement?
Using the whole play, explain your reasons for OR against this viewpoint.

Activity 7

a) As part of your preparation in the weeks leading up to the exam, select a question each week from the list. Plan your response, then write part of the essay you have planned.

b) Share your work with a partner or teacher, and ask for feedback. Amend and complete your response after listening to their advice.

SKILLS AND PRACTICE

Sample answers

Below, you will find extracts from students' answers to exam-style questions, along with examiner comments.

Sample answer 1

> 'I rang Mrs Gascoyne. I told her that you're going to take your Maths A level next year.'
>
> Explore how Stephens presents attitudes to education in the extract above and elsewhere in the play.

Firstly, in the extract from the play the playwright Simon Stephens presents Judy's attitude to education. At this point, Christopher has run away from his father's house in Swindon to find where his mother lives. However, he still wants to do his Maths exam as he has been working on it for months. Here, Judy tells Christopher that she has cancelled the exam for this year. She takes him into a park and buys him a lolly before she tells him. It's almost like she is trying to bribe a younger child into being happy before she has to say something umpleasant. This shows that she does not think his education is very important. By using the adjectives 'next year', Stephens makes Judy say that it's not necessary to do it this year. I think she believes that Christopher will understand that an exam is not very important after all he has been through recently. This shows she doesn't really know him very well now. It has been two years since she lived with him and she does not know he has changed.

Secondly, in another part of the play, we see Judy take Christopher to school to do the exam. This comes after she starts to understand that he needs the A level because he still wants to be an astronaut. You can tell she doesn't know much about his education though as Siobhan has never met her before. She says 'You must be Christopher's mother'. And Judy does not know what to say. She has not been the person to make sure that Christopher goes to school because he was living with Ed. This could suggest that she was not interested in education for him till now. As she left him two years ago, it might be a new school for him and that is why she doesn't know very much.

Stephens shows that Ed's attitude to education is different to Judy's. Ed goes to the school to argue with the headteacher about Christopher doing Maths A level. He argues with her about it and

Examiner comments:

- Provides context for the extract. Infers working for months as that is not stated in the text.
- Spelling is incorrect, but tries to use the appropriate word. Comment about the lolly is starting to support ideas about attitudes.
- Refers again to the question so still on track.
- Not completely accurate use of terminology but shows understanding that Stephens chooses words for a specific purpose.
- Comments on reason for Judy's behaviour. Indicates thought about the context of the event within the play.
- Refers to another scene to support the earlier point, extending the idea in a slightly different direction.
- Not quite correct as a quotation, but shows understanding of what the comment infers.
- Further refers to the task, still sticking to the point.
- Changes focus to Ed. Develops the answer in different way, allowing wider consideration of the question.

SKILLS AND PRACTICE

Misunderstands the conversation and the point is not quite correct.

Makes general remarks about Ed and education but does not explain ideas in enough detail.

> offers to pay for someone to sit with him to do the exams and then swears about Christopher having a crap time at school so he should be allowed to do the exam. Ed knows Christopher wants to be a scientist as they talk about things like stars and the Milky Way, so he wants him to get a good education so he can do that. Ed is a plumber and maybe he thinks Christopher will be clever enough to get a better job than him. At the end of the play, the audience finds out that Ed has also said Christopher can do his next A level in Further Maths as well. This proves that education is important to Ed.

Brings focus back to the question with reference to teachers.

Focus on exams is not quite what the question asks for. Needs more explanation to link the two ideas.

Makes a careless error in grammar – should be 'would have'.

Fair, but unexplained. Does not follow up the reference to other teachers so overall the response feels incomplete.

> There are two teachers in the play. Both of them have different attitudes to education. It is a bit weird that the headteacher seems to have a bad attitude towards exams as she first tells Ed that Christopher cannot do the A level. She claims that 'no one from school has done an exam before', which shows she does not think about how every student might need to get qualifications. Mrs Gascoyne might be showing how some teachers write off the kids they work with if they are not very clever or cannot read very well. I would of thought that if she was head of a special school she ought to have a better attitude to education than that.

This response has some clear points that are relevant to the question and identifies appropriate scenes and characters. It is quite narrative but does not explain the point of the examples provided. There are some parts where the candidate appears to have forgotten what they were going to write. Using a plan may have helped to stay on track with the answer and use the time better.

Sample answer 2

> 'Stephens presents Christopher in a way that makes the audience sympathize with him.'
>
> To what extent do you agree with this point of view?

Positive opening sets out the issues likely to make the audience sympathetic.

Reference to Stephens shows awareness that the play was written for a specific purpose.

> In the play, Stephens presents Christopher as being a person who is confused, worried, scared and alone. He wants his life to be settled and predictable but, from the very start of the play, finds that it is not what he thought. He quickly discovers that his life is far more complicated than he ever realized. Stephens shows the impact of this on Christopher through the ways he has to change and adapt to cope with unexpected situations.

SKILLS AND PRACTICE

By the end of the play, when Christopher says, 'I can do anything', the audience is ready to agree with him, but that is not the case for the whole play.

When the play opens, Christopher is seen kneeling by the side of a dead dog. This makes the audience shocked at first but then start to feel sorry for him as losing a pet is heartbreaking (I know as I had my dog put down last week ☹). Christopher is groaning and this makes the audience think he is in pain emotionally, which gets them on his side at once. When Mrs Shears swears at Christopher about the dog, this also shocks the audience as it seems unnecessary but does make you wonder if there is more to what is happening than first appears. Then, when the policeman arrives and tries to pick him up from the ground, the audience realizes that something is wrong with Christopher as he reacts in such an extreme way to being helped up. He is clearly not in physical pain but seems to be in emotional distress, which can be more hurtful on the inside. His pain may be more mental as well, which cannot be seen. So the opening scene makes the audience curious but also sympathize with Christopher because he seems to be suffering.

Stephens shows us in a number of other events that Christopher deserves our sympathy. His character is shown to be very truthful – 'I do not tell lies' – as he does not understand why people would choose to lie. This foreshadows events when he discovers that he has been lied to by the person who he trusts the most, his father. He also seems to have no mother as she died suddenly two years before. Stephens shows that he lacks emotions about that event and asks questions more about her medical history – 'was it a heart attack?' – than about her, which shows he is interested in science more than people. The audience can see how hard it is for him and his father to get along together sometimes as Ed reacts with anger and aggression when Christopher does not do what he is told. Ed shouts and even hits Christopher, which makes the audience wonder if Christopher is being abused. The reactions seem out of proportion to what Christopher has done and this is puzzling at first. But then the audience finds out that Ed was responsible for the dog's death and this breaks the trust between Christopher and his father. Stephens cleverly shows how the investigation that Christopher started was actually about his own family but that makes us sympathize with him more as we can see how damaged Christopher feels by it all. The person who he lived with and believed in has lied about all sorts of things and only really fessed up because he has been found out. I think that the last scene when Christopher and his dad are getting to know each other again is really emotional and makes you feel sorry for both of them as you can tell how much the relationship really means.

Annotations:

- Direct quotation indicates knowledge of the character and events.
- Addresses an aspect of question by showing the audience response to a specific event.
- Refers to two different sections of play, demonstrating good knowledge of events.
- Comments about character and impact on the audience show understanding of the context of the character.
- Considers other ways Stephens makes the audience sympathize with Christopher, focusing on the task.
- Uses subject terminology appropriately.
- Links characteristics with features that promote sympathy. Focuses on the question.
- Discusses the wider emotional impact of events. Needs to be linked to audience sympathy.
- Uses inappropriate slang/colloquial term.
- Mentions 'sorry for them' but does not address the question.

SKILLS AND PRACTICE

Needs better focus, though still deals with the question. Could be running out of time.

> Stephens presents Christopher as being a teenage boy with difficulties understanding people's thinking and so I agree that Stephens makes the audience want to sympathize as lots of people must have felt like that at some time even if it hasn't involved a dog being killed to make a point.

This answer includes some detailed explanation about what makes the audience sympathize but goes off the point in places. It shows good knowledge of the play through references to different parts of the text. Some comments and phrases are inconsistent with an exam response.

Sample answer 3

> Select two characters from the list below. Explain how Stephens uses them to show how Christopher changes during the course of the play.
> - Mrs Alexander
> - Siobhan
> - Roger Shears

Expands the question to show how it will be addressed in the response.

Understands that Stephens has made deliberate choices about how Christopher will be seen by the audience.

Supports the point with a quote effectively embedded into the sentence.

Subject terminology shows understanding of the structure of the play.

Provides context for later comments to demonstrate understanding about the chosen characters.

> Stephens presents changes in Christopher as he grows up during the course of the play, which allows the audience to see and understand Christopher's point of view and feelings. This essay will discuss how other characters reveal different aspects of Christopher during this maturing process. I have chosen to use Mrs Alexander and Roger Shears.
>
> At the beginning of the play, Stephens allows Christopher to be fearful initially of anyone who is not part of his immediate family. He refuses to speak to or move for the policeman, reacting aggressively and immediately to the attempt to lift him from the ground, resulting in 'arrest for assaulting a police officer'. This creates a bad first impression of Christopher for the audience and creates tension. However, he is more cooperative at the police station despite his initial hostility though he again reacts by screaming when he is touched. Through this, the audience can sense that, although Christopher is scared of unknown people, he is not incapable of learning how to deal with them. The foreshadowing here enables the audience to anticipate that Christopher will develop this skill still further as the play develops.

91

SKILLS AND PRACTICE

When Christopher meets Mrs Alexander, Stephens allows him to be quite nervous and uncertain about her. This can be seen in the way he refuses to go into her home as she is a 'stranger'. Stephens also shows Christopher to be unsure about what he is being offered to eat and drink, based on colour: 'I don't like lemon squash'. Stephens shows he is too nervous to wait for the drink and biscuits because Mrs Alexander takes so long to get them: 'I waited six minutes'. The image here is that Christopher has limited social skills and does not understand etiquette linked to receiving hospitality. This emphasizes to the audience that he is inexperienced in dealing with people he has not met before and foreshadows his difficulties when having to deal with other new people en route to London. Stephens allows Christopher to meet Mrs Alexander again when he is more inclined to return her friendliness. She challenges him about leaving, which is the first time the audience sees him having to account for his actions to anyone except Ed. Although only a small change, Stephens presents Christopher as being able to adapt to a new situation, albeit in a limited and safe way, but this indicates again that change for Christopher is inevitable. At this point, the audience cannot fully realize where this change will come from. Stephens keeps a sense of anticipation during the scene, which is raised to tension level when Mrs Alexander discloses previously unknown information about Christopher's mother.

In contrast to Mrs Alexander, who Stephens creates to be a well-meaning but rather interfering busybody, Roger Shears is presented as someone who may pose an actual threat to Christopher. He is only known of through circumstantial means during the first Act and the audience is made to wonder why Ed reacts so aggressively – 'that man is evil' – when Christopher innocently names him as his prime suspect for killing Wellington. Stephens demonstrates from the outset that his relationship with Judy is not as harmonious as might have been anticipated. They have been living together for two years and things appear to be uncertain; 'you made a fool of me' is the line directly addressed to Roger. Stephens presents him as rather thoughtless and careless of other people's feelings through his use of the word 'fool', which has connotations of being the deliberate butt of a joke and the desire to embarrass. The audience reacts to his casual disregard of the feelings of someone he is meant to care about by feeling that he is unreliable and untrustworthy. Stephens cements this impression when Roger starts to talk about Christopher in the third person… .

Annotations:
- Refers again to Stephens making the character behave in certain ways.
- Makes an interesting but irrelevant point, adding nothing to the account of the first meeting.
- Slightly inaccurate quotation, which may have been better paraphrased.
- Links comments to the whole text and the question.
- Focuses again on the question and how Stephens presents change in the character.
- Suggests the reason for the choice of second character.
- Use of appropriate vocabulary shows understanding of how the character is presented.
- Shows understanding of effects on the audience by focusing on the implications of Stephens's word choice.
- Focuses again on the context of the event before moving to show the effect on Christopher.

SKILLS AND PRACTICE

This is a carefully thought through response that addresses the question through examining how Stephens constructs the characters and situations as a whole. It returns to the question at various points and is supported effectively by well-chosen quotations and references. However, it could be improved by more attention to word use and impact.

Sample answer 4

> 'My name is Christopher John Francis Boone. I know all the countries of the world and the capital cities. And every prime number up to 7507.'
>
> Starting with this speech, explore the ways that Stephens presents ideas about difference in the whole play.

Addresses the question and focuses on Stephens's purpose in writing the play.

This play is set in the late 20th century when attitudes to difference and disability were undergoing massive change. Stephens uses the play as a commentary on how society deals with and treats difference as it is presented via the character of 15-year-old Christopher Boone.

Focuses on the quotation and starts to analyse language used to create the character.

In the speech provided, the simplistic language shows how deceptive appearances and presentation can be as Christopher shows how his obsessive interests lie mainly with himself and his abilities in recall and maths. The implication behind the statement about his identity is that facts and numbers are more important to him than other people. Stephens uses prime numbers as a metaphor for the life that Christopher leads. Each number is only divisible by itself and the number one, and Christopher could be seen in a similar way, unaffected by external factors as he faces the world alone. The focus on these numbers may also suggest that Christopher experiences loneliness as he struggles to cope with things that do not fit his world view. His knowledge of 'countries' and 'capital cities' suggests that he is aware of the world beyond his own street, but lacks any knowledge of what these places are really like. He is restricted to the facts, demonstrating no imaginative capacity to consider what life in any of those places might be like. Stephens introduces Christopher as a snapshot of a world view different to that held by most of the audience.

Moves beyond literal interpretation of what is meant to consider underlying meaning.

Explores Stephens's purpose in using a specific device, which links to the initial statement about Christopher's view of life.

Suggests deeper analysis of the text by giving an alternate interpretation.

Embedded quotations provide relevant support for the points being made.

Links comments made so far to the overall question as well as reinforcing the particular focus of the response.

Later on in the same section of the drama, Christopher provides more information about the way that his views do not concur with the majority. He states that he does 'not tell lies' as he explores the concept of figurative language and the difficulties such language gives him. He cites how a metaphor is like a lie because it compares two unrelated ideas. He is made to 'forget what the person is talking about' when he grapples with

93

SKILLS AND PRACTICE

unpicking the images created by a metaphor. Stephens focuses attention on Christopher's certainty that the truth is a matter of choice as he explodes common images foreshadowing some of the revelations to come later in the play. Christopher refers to 'skeletons in a cupboard' without realizing the irony that he will discover that his own father is hiding a number of significant facts from him. He refers to being the 'apple of their eye', a common saying indicating pride and love towards a person, which foreshadows him losing his love and respect for his father when Ed reveals his secrets. Stephens emphasizes how Christopher's limited perceptions single him out as different in his responses and expectations of those closest to him. He appears to be vulnerable, fragile and unaware of the consequences of what he is saying to Siobhan about his own situation.

[Annotation: Moves the response forward by referring to other sections, which are linked thematically with the point here.]

[Annotation: Identifies audience response, which links to earlier comments about the presentation of the character.]

However, it is not only Christopher's attitude towards the world that Stephens uses to show responses to difference in the play. Other characters represent stereotypes of how people may deal with difference. Christopher is an atypical teenager in his behaviour and understanding but he is judged by most characters solely on his appearance and therefore treated without consideration in some situations. The police officers show an almost callous disregard for his person as they 'try to lift', 'tries to take..' and 'grab' at him at different points in order to secure his compliance with their demands. Each one fails to address his need to have his personal space respected. Overall, the image Stephens creates of the police carries negative connotations about their understanding of people who do not conform in some way. Their language as they address Christopher as 'little shit' or 'monkey' further reinforces Stephens's presentation of them as unprofessional with no respect for this vulnerable young person.

[Annotation: Indicates the ability to see characters as creations by Stephens to make a point about a particular issue.]

[Annotation: Quotations from different points support the premise, showing excellent grasp of theme and the ability to explore the overall impression created.]

[Annotation: Explores language choices to develop the earlier point in a different direction.]

This response focuses on a particular feature of the question and how that is shown by Stephens across a number of different sections and situations. It shows excellent use of embedded textual references, which support points and demonstrate understanding of underlying ideas. Subject terminology is used appropriately and demonstrates the ability to explore Stephens's methods.